Editor
Eric Migliaccio

Editor in Chief
Karen J. Goldfluss, M.S. Ed.

Cover Artist
Barb Lorseyedi

Illustrator
Mark Mason

Art Coordinator
Renée Mc Elwee

Imaging
James Edward Grace
Craig Gunnell

Publisher

Mary D. Smith, M.S. Ed.

Project-Based Writing

Grade 3

TCR 2781

- Pre-made & customizable units
- Multi-genre lessons & projects
- Targeting 21st-century skills
- Technology-based lessons
- Cross-curricular connections
- Guided by student choice

Teacher Created Resources

Author
Heather Wolpert-Gawron

For information about Common Core State Standards, see pages 4–5 of this book or visit *http://www.teachercreated.com/standards*

Teacher Created Resources
6421 Industry Way
Westminster, CA 92683
www.teachercreated.com

ISBN: 978-1-4206-2781-7

© 2014 Teacher Created Resources
Made in U.S.A.

Teacher Created Resources

Table of Contents

Table of Contents *(cont.)*

Common Core State Standards

Project-Based Writing, Grade 3 gives students and teachers the necessary resources and ideas needed in the process of creating project-based writing units in the classroom. During each step of this process, students will engage in activities that meet one or more of the following Common Core State Standards. (©Copyright 2010. National Governors Association Center for Best Practices and Council of Chief State School Officers. All rights reserved.) For more information about the Common Core State Standards, go to *http://www.corestandards.org/* or visit *http://www.teachercreated.com/standards*.

Informational Text Standards

Key Ideas and Details

ELA.RI.3.1. Ask and answer questions to demonstrate understanding of a text, referring explicitly to the text as the basis for the answers.

ELA.RI.3.2. Determine the main idea of a text; recount the key details and explain how they support the main idea.

ELA.RI.3.3. Describe the relationship between a series of historical events, scientific ideas or concepts, or steps in technical procedures in a text, using language that pertains to time, sequence, and cause/effect.

Craft and Structure

ELA.RI.3.4. Determine the meaning of general academic and domain-specific words and phrases in a text relevant to a grade 3 topic or subject area.

ELA.RI.3.5. Use text features and search tools (e.g., key words, sidebars, hyperlinks) to locate information relevant to a given topic efficiently.

ELA.RI.3.6. Distinguish their own point of view from that of the author of a text.

Integration of Knowledge and Ideas

ELA.RI.3.7. Use information gained from illustrations (e.g., maps, photographs) and the words in a text to demonstrate understanding of the text (e.g., where, when, why, and how key events occur).

ELA.RI.3.8. Describe the logical connection between particular sentences and paragraphs in a text (e.g., comparison, cause/effect, first/second/third in a sequence).

ELA.RI.3.9. Compare and contrast the most important points and key details presented in two texts on the same topic.

Range of Reading and Level of Text Complexity

ELA.RI.3.10. By the end of the year, read and comprehend informational texts, including history/social studies, science, and technical texts, at the high end of the grades 2–3 text complexity band independently and proficiently.

Foundational Skills Standards

Phonics and Word Recognition

ELA.RF.3.3. Know and apply grade-level phonics and word-analysis skills in decoding words.

Fluency

ELA.RF.3.4. Read with sufficient accuracy and fluency to support comprehension.

Common Core State Standards *(cont.)*

Writing Standards

Text Types and Purposes

ELA.W.3.1. Write opinion pieces on topics or texts, supporting a point of view with reasons.

ELA.W.3.2. Write informative/explanatory texts to examine a topic and convey ideas and information clearly.

ELA.W.3.3. Write narratives to develop real or imagined experiences or events using effective technique, descriptive details, and clear event sequences.

Production and Distribution of Writing

ELA.W.3.4. With guidance and support from adults, produce writing in which the development and organization are appropriate to task and purpose.

ELA.W.3.5. With guidance and support from peers and adults, develop and strengthen writing as needed by planning, revising, and editing.

ELA.W.3.6. With guidance and support from adults, use technology to produce and publish writing (using keyboarding skills) as well as to interact and collaborate with others.

Research to Build and Present Knowledge

ELA.W.3.7. Conduct short research projects that build knowledge about a topic.

ELA.W.3.8. Recall information from experiences or gather information from print and digital sources; take brief notes on sources and sort evidence into provided categories.

ELA.W.3.9. Draw evidence from literary or informational texts to support analysis, reflection, and research.

Range of Writing

ELA.W.3.10. Write routinely over extended time frames (time for research, reflection, and revision) and shorter time frames (a single sitting or a day or two) for a range of discipline-specific tasks, purposes, and audiences.

Speaking and Listening Standards

Comprehension and Collaboration

ELA.SL.3.1. Engage effectively in a range of collaborative discussions (one-on-one, in groups, and teacher-led) with diverse partners on grade 3 topics and texts, building on others' ideas and expressing their own clearly.

Presentation of Knowledge and Ideas

ELA.SL.3.4. Report on a topic or text, tell a story, or recount an experience with appropriate facts and relevant, descriptive details, speaking clearly at an understandable pace.

ELA.SL.3.5. Add visual displays when appropriate to emphasize or enhance certain facts or details.

Introduction: Nothing Fits in a Box Anymore

This book and the concepts contained within it are a direct response to the growing trend toward differentiation and individualization. The multi-genre, hybrid approach of *Project-Based Writing* recognizes the differences between students, how they learn, and how they seek to show their learning. It caters to their individual strengths, while also guiding them toward the exploration of other means of expression that they might instinctively tend to avoid.

Ultimately, project-based writing is about choice. Just as we live in a culture in which every person in the coffee line can have his or her own personalized beverage made to order, so, too, should students be given the tools and the opportunity to show off their knowledge in many different ways.

A vital aspect of project-based writing is the blending of school life with real life. Often, there is a disconnect between the two. Many students, especially tweens and teens, see school life as totally separate from life outside of school. Therefore, it becomes our job as teachers to make sure that the classroom more directly correlates to the outside world. Choice is a huge part of doing that. So whenever possible in your curriculum, you should feel encouraged to offer student choice, while of course still emphasizing academic rigor and content knowledge.

The multi-genre activities and units covered in *Project-Based Writing* offer the best of both worlds: students gain a functional knowledge of a whole slew of genres, formats, and ways of expressing themselves; and at the same time, they learn to successfully weave these separate elements together into a cohesive whole that digs deeper into the topics, themes, and issues that are most important to their lives outside of school. It is this step of integration that moves students beyond the simple regurgitation of ideas and into a higher level of thinking: that of creation.

How To Use This Book

This book is divided into four parts, each designed to help you, the teacher, guide your students in the creation of project-based writing units.

I. Project-Based Writing and the Multi-Genre Approach (pages 9–12)

Here is where you can find an overview of the ideas behind project-based writing and why the multi-genre approach is so vital to engaging your students and enriching their writing.

II. Creating a Project-Based Writing Unit (pages 13–18)

This section shows you how to begin the process of introducing your students to multi-genre projects. This is where you and your students can start to hone in on the topics and themes that most interest them. It's also where you will learn about the elements that make up each project-based writing unit and where you'll get a glimpse at what a finished product could look like.

III. Resources (pages 19–57)

The resources contained within this section are divided into four main categories:

Activities   **Research**   **Organization**   **Assessment**

Collectively — or in any combination you choose — these resources are intended to provide your students with the tools needed to produce projects that are effective, engaging, and unique. Each page is written to the students, and each is designed to serve as a resource your students can refer back to as they work through the creative process. Each new resource in this section begins with a brief statement explaining how it can be helpful in the creation of a project-based writing unit.

A. Activities

Here you'll find the nuts and bolts of any project-based writing unit. These activities are varied and flexible; they span several genres and skills, and they can be introduced in any order. The aim here is to equip your students with an abundance of options and ideas.

B. Research

This section gives your students practical methods for conducting and recording the research they will need to do in order to dig deeper into their topics.

How To Use This Book *(cont.)*

III. Resources *(cont.)*

C. Organization

Students need to pre-plan and structure their work so that they stay focused and on task. The checklists and multiple outlines provided here will help do just that.

D. Assessment

Need a rubric? There are options for different rubrics in this section, as well as a guide to help your students design their own rubrics. Also included is a form that students can use to record your feedback in their own words.

IV. Pre-Made Project-Based Writing Units (pages 58–96)

Finally, this book includes four pre-made project-based writing units that you can use as is, from beginning to end.

For grade 3, the four pre-made units are as follows:

Teach the Teacher

Persuasive-Writing Project

Create a City

Create a School

Each unit begins with an overview page that provides step-by-step instructions on how to proceed through the unit. You can also dip into the "Activities" section to add or swap out any lesson you wish. It is this ability to interchange lessons and create different combinations of units that makes this concept of project-based writing with a multi-genre emphasis so unique.

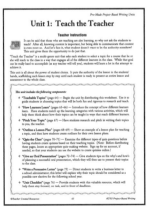

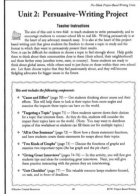

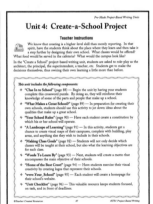

What Is Project-Based Writing?

Project-based writing puts a spin on the concept of project-based learning, which is the act of learning through identifying a real-world problem and developing its solution. The project that results from this endeavor encourages students to use critical-thinking skills to journey towards an authentic goal.

Project-based writing activities strive to meet certain criteria. By design, these activities are . . .

❖ multi-genre.

❖ differentiated.

❖ thematic.

❖ both linguistic and non-linguistic.

❖ cross-curricular.

❖ based on real-world scenarios.

❖ guided by student choice.

❖ filled with 21st-century connections.

Project-based writing argues that any subject — be it language arts or STEM — can benefit from strong writing practice. Any genre of writing can support the other. And any engaging activity that links academic learning to the real world can be a 21st-century tool.

10 Reasons to Teach Project-Based Writing

1. It is an organic way to integrate all core subjects — math, science, history, and language arts.

2. It proves to students that imagination and creativity are connected to research and expository writing.

3. It hits all the major elements of the higher levels of Bloom's Taxonomy: Analysis, Evaluation, and Creation.

4. By allowing students to choose their format of showing what they know, the buy-in for the quality of the final project is tremendous.

5. Students develop projects that are individualized, unique, and specific from each other.

6. It is a powerful way to incorporate all multiple intelligences: visual, verbal, logical, musical, physical, social, solitary, and naturalistic.

7. It desegregates nonfiction and fiction, blending the two.

8. It integrates the core subjects with non-core subjects, potentially using technology, art, music, etc.

9. It is a rigorous assessment requiring high levels of thought and communication.

10. It requires use of the entire writing process — from brainstorming to revising, editing, and completing the final draft — regardless of the genres picked and the topic chosen.

The Multi-Genre Approach

At the heart of project-based writing is the concept of melding multiple genres into a final product. This multi-genre approach involves taking several distinct types of writing and fusing them into something unique and powerful. Essentially, a hybrid is created.

Throughout history, humans have strived to create hybrids. In science, people have bred their ideal loyal companion in the Golden Retriever or created their perfect salad accessory in the bug-resistant tomato. In literature, authors and storytellers have written about hybrids, such as the unicorn and Pegasus.

Here are some examples of hybrids throughout history:

Picture	Description
	half electric, half gasoline-powered
	half person, half fish
	half Labrador, half poodle
	half chocolate, half peanut butter

In project-based writing, a hybrid is created when we combine genres that revolve around a shared topic or theme. The result is a multi-genre project that uses the best of different presentations and weaves them together into a totally new creature.

After all, just as any subject can benefit from strong writing practice, so can any genre of writing help support another. The multi-genre aspect of project-based writing is important because it is vital that students understand that genres are not compartmentalized in life. For example, a narrative can support a persuasive argument, just as a graph can support a summary. Weaving the strengths of multiple genres together into one project is the key to project-based writing and to providing one's audience with a richer, fuller picture of a topic or theme.

Differentiation in Education

As you know, there are many different kinds of learners out there in the classrooms. Some students like to write, others like to sing; some like to play sports, while others like to draw. A multi-genre approach allows students to choose ways to show off what they know and what they've learned about a topic, using the methods that are the most interesting to them. Just as importantly, it allows them to challenge themselves and present topics using methods that are not normally in their nature to attempt. So by requiring students to display their content knowledge in multiple ways, you are allowing them to operate within their comfort zones on the one hand, while also pushing them to more fully develop a technique that is challenging to them.

21st-Century Connection: Many students know what interests them, what kind of learner they are, and how they most like to display their knowledge. But it's also very empowering for them to take quizzes that help them identify their natural instincts. With that in mind, consider having students take a test to identify the style in which they learn best. One such four-part quiz is available at The George Lucas Foundation's website, Edutopia.org:

http://www.edutopia.org/multiple-intelligences-learning-styles-quiz

PAGE 1 OF 4

How much time do you spend:

	NONE	ONLY A LITTLE	A FAIR AMOUNT	A LOT	ALL THE TIME
Getting lost in a good book.	○	○	○	○	○
Doing crafts or arts projects.	○	○	○	○	○
Trying to solve mysteries, riddles, or crossword puzzles.	○	○	○	○	○
Writing a journal or blogging.	○	○	○	○	○
Reflecting on your life and your future.	○	○	○	○	○
Playing sports.	○	○	○	○	○
Yearning to spend time with nature.	○	○	○	○	○

(Next Page >)

See page 12 for a complete breakdown of the different types of learners that you may have in your classroom.

Differentiation in Education *(cont.)*

Because we hear so much about differentiation in education, let's take a moment to look more closely at the different ways people learn—and just as importantly for purposes of project-based writing, the different ways people best show what they've learned. This information is usually referred to as "multiple intelligences." Consult the following chart:

The Multiple Intelligences	Some Ways They Learn/Show What They Know
Visual/Spatial	puzzles, maps, 3-D models, charts, graphs, architecture
Verbal/Linguistic	reading, word games, poetry, speeches, lectures
Logical/Mathematical	patterns, puzzles, experiments, investigations, mysteries
Musical/Auditory	songs, lyrics, rhythmic speaking, dance, musical instruments
Physical/Kinesthetic	movement, hands-on activities, acting out, role-playing, realia
Social/Interpersonal	interaction, dialogue, group dynamics, e-mail, video conferencing
Solitary/Intrapersonal	introspection, diaries, journals, books, independent study
Naturalistic	walks; digging; collecting; using microscopes, telescopes, maps, and globes

Choosing a Topic or Theme

The first step a student must take in creating a project-based writing unit is choosing a topic that piques his or her interest. When thinking about a topic, the student might want to choose one with which he or she is somewhat familiar but could learn more about through research. On the other hand, the student could choose a topic he or she has always wanted to know more about but hasn't had the opportunity to explore in detail.

An ideal topic could be anything from a historical event or person to a hot-topic issue that the student wishes to advocate for or argue against.

A theme-based project is another option to consider. Themes, however, can often be discovered and uncovered midway through a topic-based project.

Where to Find Topics

Topics are always out there, ready to be dissected and discussed. Here are just a few of the many possibilities you can present to your students:

- ❖ **Historical Events or People** — Native Americans • American Revolution • Declaration of Independence • Underground Railroad • Emancipation Proclamation • The Trail of Tears • The Louisiana Purchase • Trojan War • Eruption of Mt. Vesuvius • Abraham Lincoln • Ferdinand Magellan • Julius Caesar • Queen Elizabeth • Susan B. Anthony • Sacagawea

- ❖ **Writers/Artists/Scientists** — Leonardo da Vinci • Michelangelo • Donatello • William Shakespeare • Galileo • Copernicus • Lamarck • Kepler

- ❖ **Recent Events or People** — September 11, 2001 • The Dot-Com Bubble • The Housing Boom and Crash • Bill Gates • Barack Obama • Lance Armstrong • Muhammad Ali • Danica Patrick • Hurricane Katrina • Japan Earthquake and Tsunami of 2011

See page 14 for a great way to create a collaborative classroom resource library!

- ❖ **Advocacy Issues** — Paying Students for Grades or Attendance • Global Warming • School Budgets • Cloning • Dress Code • Gum Chewing • Cell-Phone Usage • Autism • Eating Disorders

- ❖ **Themes** — Change • Courage • Acceptance • Loyalty • Success • Aging • Overcoming Adversity

- ❖ **Morals** — "Beauty is only skin deep." • "Birds of a feather flock together." • "Live and let live." • "Look before you leap."

You may choose to present these to your class, or you could opt for topics that align more closely with your class's curriculum. A list of possible topics could serve as a way to jumpstart your students' thought processes about what kinds of subjects would provide the basis for dynamic project-based writing units.

The Student-Created Resource Library

It's true that you can use the traditional way of having students find their sources, research their topics, and collect their data. But instead, consider making research a collaborative, community-building project for the entire classroom.

Imagine an area of the classroom filled with the resources brought in by the students. As students discover reference material, articles, and chapters from outside the classroom, they bring copies of the material into the classroom and file them in this location for other students to use.

It's easy to start. First, assign a typical advocacy topic that can be found in many different formats. Take, for example, the topic of global warming. Okay, so you've asked students to bring in copies of articles, book pages, etc., all on global warming. Create a file called "Global Warming" and place it in a special file box called "Resource Library." File all of the resources into it.

Try it as a weekly current-events assignment leading up to a research report. It's possible that by the time the students have to actually select a topic, you will have a resource library already underway for that topic.

The great part of this is that it's a growing, dynamic library. As kids settle on their topics, they continue to research and add to the files.

In addition, to encourage further collaboration, keep a chart in the classroom with everyone's names and selected topics so that when students come across research that relates to a peer's topic, they can refer that student to the evidence they found. It's a collaborative form of research that uses the classroom as a working, growing reference library.

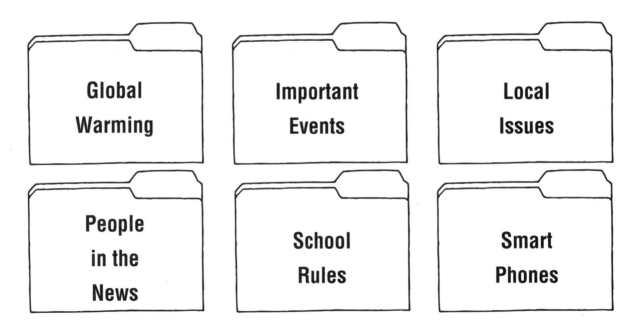

What Are the Parts of a Unit?

In order to create a project-based writing unit, students will use many skills and work in multiple genres. They will do this in all of the steps of the creation process, from planning and research to writing and the production of a final project. This final product will consist of two basic parts: the multi-genre elements and the container.

> *See page 18 for examples of containers and the multi-genre elements they could contain.*

The Multi-Genre Elements

Once students choose the topic or theme on which they will build their projects, they next should begin to think about what elements will make up their final project. These multi-genre elements will comprise the bulk of the project, and they will ideally be a mixture of multiple written and visual genres. In order to really challenge themselves (and also explore more nuances of their topics and themes), students should work not just with the elements with which they are most comfortable. While a visual learner is encouraged to use all of the elements that align with his or her instinctual abilities (say, creating comic books and designing website homepages), that student is also expected to consider penning a persuasive essay or crafting a campaign speech that further illuminates the topic.

A list of possible multi-genre elements is included on the following page. While there is some overlap, the elements are divided into columns depending on whether they are primarily written or visual. You may wish to copy this list and distribute one

> *Many of these elements are explored individually and in greater detail on pages 19–45 of the "Activities" section.*

to each student. Have your students examine each column and circle those activities that they may find interesting to create and that will best illustrate their chosen issue or topic. Also, allow students to add new ideas to the list. As long as the element enriches their project, students should be encouraged to let their imaginations soar.

The Container

One important guiding principle for students to keep in mind is that a project's final appearance will function best if it reflects the theme or subject that it is based on. An appropriate container will go a long way in accomplishing this. Whether it is simple or elaborate, it should function as the final piece that ties all of the other pieces together. Think of the container as the visual delivery system for the project.

A List of Multi-Genre Elements

Directions: Below are lists of possible elements you can combine for use in a project. Examine each column and circle the ones that you may find interesting to create and that will best illustrate your chosen issue or topic. If any other ideas occur to you, record them in the spaces at the bottom of the appropriate column.

Written (Linguistic)	Visual (Non-Linguistic)	Other
Campaign Speech	Advertisement	Directions
Character Sketch	Family Tree	Recipe
Dialogue	Greeting Card	Quiz
Essay	Website	How-to Guide
Fable or Fairy Tale	Picture Book	List
Website	Map	Song
Poetry	Postcard	Dance
Diary Entry	Movie Poster	Board Game
Blog	Diorama	Computer Game
Memoir	Flip Book	Reader's Theater
News Article	Building-Blocks Structure	Podcast
Op-ed Piece	Statue	Video
Petition	Comic Book	Monologue
Advocacy Essay	Comic Life (using iLife suite)	
Letters	Prezi	
Review	PowerPoint	
Script	Blueprint (using Google Sketch-up)	
Glossary		
Narrative		
Interview		
Legend		
Letter of Complaint		
Summary		

Using a Unit Checklist

A checklist is an effective organizational tool that can help students remember what's due and when. There are many different ways to format a checklist. The four pre-made units in this workbook (pages 58–96), for example, contain checklists that are tailored to those projects.

The sample checklist below can give you an idea of appropriate expectations you could have for each student to include in his or her writing unit. For the project below, you may instruct students that the top three assignments must be included. From there, they could be asked to choose one activity from each of the other categories, ensuring that the completed project contains seven pieces in all. This is just one way to approach assigning a unit's components.

Note: A blank checklist is provided on page 55 in the "Resources" section.

Date Due	Date Completed	Assigned Element	Possibilities
		Persuasive Pitch to Teacher About Topic	❖ Letter ❖ Essay
		Research	❖ Cornell Notes ❖ Quickwrites ❖ Movement Survey
		Bibliography/Works Cited	❖ n/a
		Written Piece	❖ Narrative ❖ Poem ❖ Glossary/Dictionary ❖ Interview/Dialogue ❖ Biography ❖ Diary Entry
		Visual or Technological Element	❖ Poster/Ad ❖ Cartoon ❖ PowerPoint/Prezi ❖ Website ❖ Board Game
		Mathematical Piece	❖ Map ❖ Recipe ❖ Step-by-Step Guide
		Musical- or Movement-Based Piece	❖ Cover Song ❖ Original Song ❖ Dance

What Will a Completed Project Look Like?

So what should a completed project-based writing unit look like? The short answer is that there is no one design for how these units should look. In fact, the hope is that each student project looks unique in its display and is specific in its content. Individuality is not only encouraged, it is essential to the concept. Here are some examples:

Project Topic/Theme: Childhood Obesity   **Container/Format:** Pizza Box

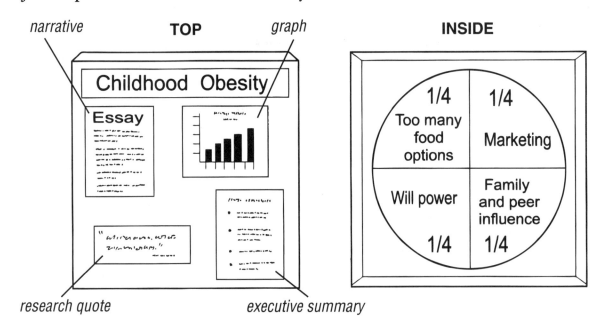

Project Topic/Theme: Pollution   **Container/Format:** Tri-Board Display

Includes: *a research paper on pollution, a science-fiction narrative about a future in which the world has been taken over by trash, comic-book frames illustrating key moments from the narrative, a recipe of the ingredients that make up a dump site, a student-created quiz, the answers to which can be found in the contents of the project*

Playing Think–Tac–Toe

 Project-Based Writing Connection: Use this resource as a brainstorming activity or to help you begin rough drafts for your projects.

Get your creative juices flowing by using these prompts to write about your topic.

Directions: Pick three prompts in a row — either down, across, or diagonally. Follow the directions, and use a seperate piece of paper for your responses.

	Narrative	**Response to Literature**	**Persuasive**
Row 1	Write a story in which the main character is brave.	Find an essay, poem, or piece of art connected to your topic and respond to the author's main message.	Take a stance on your topic and create an ad that displays your stance.
Row 2	Write a story that begins in the middle of an action-packed scene related to your topic.	Find a blog, letter, column, or poem connected to your issue. Rewrite it any way you want. Then write a note explaining what you changed and why.	In a one-page essay, take a stance on your topic and persuade the reader to agree with you.
Row 3	Make up a fairy tale about your topic. Include a moral or lesson at the end.	Find a story, poem, or piece of art connected to your topic and respond to the main character's traits.	Write a persuasive letter to your school principal about your topic.

Getting a Reader's Attention

> **Project-Based Writing Connection:** When adding a written component to your project, use a hook to grab your reader's attention right from the start.

A *hook* is that first moment of a paper — be it a narrative or an essay — that catches the reader's attention and makes him or her want to read more.

Below is a list of hooks using different strategies to begin the same story, a piece called "The First Time I Saw the Ocean." As you can see, there are many ways to hook a reader.

Fact/Statistic It was June 28 when I first saw the ocean.	**Simile/Metaphor** The white crash of the waves looked as soft as cotton, and I felt the spray cooling me like a shower.
In the Middle of the Action As the wave lifted me off of my feet and tumbled me to the shore, I tried not to laugh out loud.	**Definition** On a summer day, a beach is a really hot place with a lot of sand and tons of people.
Dialogue "It seems to stretch on forever," I exclaimed in awe. The ocean was so much bigger than I thought it was going to be.	**Onomatopoeia** Crash! Sma-bash! The waves slammed into the shore with a loud force.

Directions: After reading each of the examples above, think of an essay you are working on. You may be revising or just beginning. Try to start the piece of writing using each of these strategies. Then, pass your new list of hooks to your classmate or to an adult family member. Have him or her circle the three he or she feels are the strongest. Pick one of these three hooks to use when writing or revising.

Building Better Sentences

Project-Based Writing Connection: By varying sentence length, you can create a rhythm and a flow to your writing.

How can sentences be like roller coasters? Well, some are long and curvy and wrap around, while others are short and fast and dart about. If an entire roller coaster were made up of one kind of experience, it might get boring or predictable. To keep riders on their toes, so to speak, a good roller coaster dips and darts and builds tension. So do great stories and great research papers.

Directions: To learn a little about what it feels like to write long and short sentences and how they add to the texture in an essay, you are going to be asked to complete two strange paragraphs. Both paragraphs will be about pizza. Follow the instructions given in each box to make these two completely different paragraphs about the same topic. Use a separate piece of paper for each.

Paragraph #1

Paragraph #1 should be one sentence long. That's all. But this sentence should go on and on. Use this paragraph to write down all of your thoughts on pizza, but do not use punctuation of any kind until you get to the end. This "paragraph" should be at least a half a page long.

Paragraph #2

Paragraph #2 should also be about a half a page long. This paragraph, however, should be made up of many short sentences. These sentences must be full sentences that contain both a subject and a predicate. But here's the tough part: each sentence can be no longer than five words total.

Now that you have written both of these paragraphs, use a highlighter to mark the parts of the long sentence that you like. Maybe it's a line or two. Maybe it's just a phrase. Then, use a highlighter and indicate the best short sentences that you've written.

Now it's time to create Paragraph #3. This paragraph should be made up of the best parts of Paragraphs #1 and #2. You must use proper punctuation for this draft. Also be sure to use transition words (*however, therefore, thus,* etc.) to make your paragraph flow smoothly. Write Paragraph #3 on the back of this page or on a separate piece of paper.

Adding Extra Action

Project-Based Writing Connection: By replacing dull verbs with more active ones, you can paint a clearer, fuller picture with your words.

When writing a story, it's important to make sure that each word has personality. Each word must help your reader really see the action that is unfolding in your head.

Here's an example of a sentence that does not do that:

❖ *Ryan walked to the store.*

Can you see *how* Ryan walked to the store? No, but if you use a more specific action verb, the sentence suddenly comes alive:

❖ *Ryan ran to the store.*   ❖ *Ryan skipped to the store.*

❖ *Ryan shuffled to the store.*   ❖ *Ryan huffed and puffed to the store.*

Directions: In the following activity, cross out each verb that seems a bit boring or ordinary. Then, rewrite the new paragraph. Inject some action-packed action verbs in the places where you have removed the ordinary ones. Make sure your new paragraph still makes sense and has a good flow to it.

Original Paragraph

Beatrice hit the ball and went toward first base. She ran fast, but the first baseman picked up the ball and stepped on the base. "You're out!" the umpire said. Beatrice slowly walked back to the bench and sat next to her teammates. Paul looked at her, angry. John touched Paul's arm and said, "Hey, it was a good try. You'll get 'em next time, Bea!"

Use this space to think of some verbs that show more action. Then rewrite the paragraph on the back of your paper.

_____

_____

_____

_____

Waking Up Your Words

 Project-Based Writing Connection: Appeal to your readers' senses when you write. This will liven up your writing and keep your readers interested.

Sometimes you just need to wake up your writing and help it come alive. What if you can really make your readers see and feel what you are trying to say? That would be better than just telling them something.

For example, you could write a plain sentence like . . .

❖ I waited for the dentist.

Or, you could help your readers feel as if they're right there with you:

❖ As I waited for the dentist, my forehead dripped with sweat. When the nurse called my name, I swallowed with a loud "Gulp!"

One trick this last sentence uses is that it appeals to the senses. Here are the senses:

- sound
- sight
- smell

- taste
- touch
- feeling (like with your heart)

Directions: Take a plain sentence and make it interesting. Appeal to the senses. Here is the sentence to begin with: **I don't like broccoli.** The first one has been done for you.

1. Rewrite the sentence using **smell**. _I hate broccoli because it smells like rotten_ _garbage left out in the sun._

2. Rewrite the sentence using **sight**. _____

_____

3. Rewrite the sentence using **taste**. _____

_____

4. Rewrite the sentence using **touch**. _____

_____

Paraphrasing vs. Summarizing

 Project-Based Writing Connection: Paraphrasing and summarizing are vital skills to master. Each will help you create unique writing pieces for any project.

Summarizing and *paraphrasing* are two different skills, each with its own purpose. Think of them this way:

❖ **S**ummarizing is **s**horter. You only use the main idea from the piece.

❖ **P**araphrasing **p**uts it into your own words, sentence by sentence.

Directions: Begin by reading the paragraph about Atlantis. Then follow the directions below to show the difference between paraphrasing and summarizing.

> Atlantis is a city of great mystery. Legend has it that it sank beneath the ocean off the coast of Greece. The city, its art, and its buildings disappeared. Despite the legend, the city has never been found. Scientists and treasure-hunters have tried. However, nobody knows if Atlantis is simply a story or a mystery waiting to be solved.

Now fill out the chart below about the story you have just read.

Summarize	Paraphrase

Squeezing a Summary

Project-Based Writing Connection: Summarizing helps you persuade a reader, analyze an argument, or move a story along. It's a skill that aids many genres.

Directions: In the following activity, you are going to challenge yourself to squeeze a piece of writing down to its bare essentials. The rules are as follows:

1. The initial paragraph must be stripped down to fit in the space provided below.

2. First, cross out information that you feel is too specific to be an important detail.

3. You must use your own words.

4. You must use complete sentences.

Here is the initial paragraph:

> *In April 1906, a huge earthquake hit the city of San Francisco. From Oregon to Los Angeles, people could feel the ground shake. As a result of the earthquake, many fires started spreading throughout the city. It was a scary day for San Francisco. Eventually, however, the city was rebuilt, and it became stronger and better than ever.*

Now squeeze the key information from the paragraph into this box:

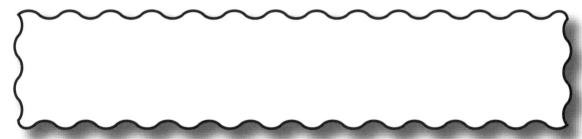

Added Challenge: Take it a step further. Cross out most of the details until only the most essential information remains. Fit what you have left inside this new box.

Creating Reading Hybrids

Project-Based Writing Connection: By fusing elements of two or more genres, you can create a new form of writing to help get your message across.

A reading hybrid takes two genres and smooshes them into one. Like Dr. Frankenstein, you will be creating a creature stitched together from different parts.

Directions: Complete the form below. After doing so, use the answers you have given to write a short story. Your short story will be a combination of two genres.

Step 1: Begin by choosing two genres from the following list. Circle your choices.

❖ Drama	❖ Mythology	❖ Science Fiction
❖ Comedy	❖ Fairy Tale	❖ Historical Fiction
❖ Mystery	❖ Fantasy	❖ Autobiography

Step 2: Now, answer questions about the two genres you chose.

Name two characteristics of Genre #1. _____

_____

Name two characteristics of Genre #2. _____

_____

Step 3: Next, come up with answers to the following questions about the story you will be writing. Use your imagination, and have fun!

Where is your story set? _____

What is the name of your main character(s)? _____

What do(es) your main character(s) look like? _____

What is the conflict in your story? _____

_____

If there is one, what is the name of the villain/bad guy, and what does he or she look like?

_____

What will be the climax (the most exciting part) of the story? _____

_____

Mixing in a Moral

Project-Based Writing Connection: Throughout your project, mix in a moral that sums up your work. This will help hammer home your point.

Have you ever learned a lesson just from reading a story? If so, the author of that story may have intentionally included a moral. A moral is a message. It's like a theme that can sum up the meaning of a story in one, easy-to-remember sentence or phrase.

Here are some morals that you can build a story around. Do they sound familiar to you?

A. It's okay to be different.

B. Never judge a book by its cover.

C. Nothing is permanent; everything changes.

D. Treat others the way you want to be treated.

Directions: Look at each of the project parts described below. Can you match the morals above to each of them? Write the letter of the moral on the line next to the description.

_____ **1.** We may think of mosquitos as small, annoying pests, but they are actually the deadliest animals on Earth! In many underdeveloped countries, mosquitos are the cause of millions of deaths. Through their tiny bites, they transmit terrible diseases to humans and other animals.

_____ **2.** The drawing on the left shows the quiet, dusty town of San Francisco in 1847, just before the California Gold Rush attracted crowds of people to the area. The picture on the right shows San Francisco today, a bustling city that nearly a million people call home.

_____ **3.** During the Civil War, Dorothea Dix became the head of the North's nursing service. However, Dix and her team of nurses treated wounded soldiers from both the North and the South. She supported the North, but she felt that all wounded soldiers deserved to be helped.

_____ **4.** The platypus is a unique animal that has the bill of a duck, the tail of a beaver, and the feet of an otter. It is also the only mammal that can lay eggs.

Perfecting the Paragraph

Project-Based Writing Connection: Effective writing often stems from organization and practice. Use this activity to help you achieve both.

When you are writing a paragraph, you need to make it "sing" — not only that, you want your singing to be in tune, and with perfect pitch. Below is an outline of a pitch-perfect paragraph.

I. Main Topic Sentence — This states what the paragraph is going to be about.

II. Evidence — This states proof about what you've said. It can be in the form of an example, a quote, a statistic, etc.

III. Commentary Sentence(s) — Here is where you put the evidence in your own words and relate it to something else you know.

IV. Concluding Sentence — Here's the place to wrap everything up.

Directions: Below is a paragraph a student has written entitled "Why I Deserve an 'A'." Use this color-coded key to underline or highlight the parts of the paragraph:

* Main Topic Sentence = **red**
* Evidence Sentence(s) = **yellow**
* Commentary Sentence(s) = **orange**
* Conclusion Sentence = **blue**

> I deserve an "A" because of the effort it took to write my last assignment. I researched different birds in the rainforests, described their habitats, and looked at their declining numbers as humans chop down the trees. I was very specific in my Internet searches. For instance, when I first typed in "rainforests," I received 7,480,000 results. I put more thought into what I was doing, and I made my search more specific. Using an Advanced Search tool, I typed in "birds of the Brazilian rainforests." My results dipped down to 37,000. Of course, I didn't look through all of those, but it became much easier to find what I wanted. Not only did I learn a lot about the birds, but I began to feel for them, too. They are beautiful, and their homes are threatened. In the end, I believe my essay deserves an "A" because my effort can be seen in my paper's quality.

Perfecting the Paragraph *(cont.)*

Teacher Directions: The following activity can show students how to take the parts of a paragraph and assemble them into something that really sings. Begin by making copies of the sentences and cutting them into strips. Then instruct students to mix and match the sentences until they are in the correct order. The result will form a pitch-perfect paragraph about Atlanta, Georgia.

Atlanta, Georgia, was founded in 1837.

Its population has grown a lot since it was named for a young girl in the 1800s.

Back then, it was called Marthasville in honor of the then-governor's daughter, and it had only about 30 people living there.

Now it has close to 5 million people in its metropolitan area; and with its ties to both tradition and modern innovation, it is now the hub of the New South.

Wow, Atlanta has come a really long way since it was named after little Martha!

Finding a Poem

 Project-Based Writing Connection: By repeating a key line throughout your project, you can create a found poem that ties the elements together.

A *found poem* combines your original poetry with a repeating line that is not very poem-like. To create a found poem, you first have to "find" a phrase that you believe really rings true to the heart of your project's topic or theme. You can find lines like that in many unusual places. Here are just a few spots to look:

❖ directions	❖ references	❖ catalogues
❖ recipes	❖ ads	❖ textbooks
❖ horoscopes	❖ letters	❖ cartoons
❖ fortune cookies	❖ e-mails	❖ cereal boxes

For example, let's say you are studying American history and are writing a poem that describes some aspect of the American Revolution. In your search for inspiration, you go into your pantry at home and look at a box of breakfast cereal. The phrase "A Great Way to Wake Up in the Morning" catches your eye. What would a poem based on that phrase look like? How could you tie in that phrase with your historical topic? That's the challenge of creating a found poem.

Directions: Follow each step below to create a found poem.

Step 1: Begin by choosing one of these topics:

❖ parents	❖ video games	❖ cell phones
❖ chores	❖ allergies	❖ homework

Step 2: You will next need to find a phrase to repeat throughout your poem. Look anywhere in the classroom for your inspiration. Look at the posters on the walls, flip through your textbook, or search through the classroom library. All it takes is one phrase to catch your eye and capture your imagination. Write your phrase here:

_____

Step 3: On a separate piece of paper, write a poem with at least two stanzas. Stay focused on your topic, but also remember to pepper your phrase throughout your poem. By combining these two elements — your topic and your phrase — you can create an interesting and unique final product.

Shaping a Poem

Project-Based Writing Connection: Use the idea of a shape poem to create a unique piece on your topic.

A *shape poem* is a way to combine what you know about symbols with what you know about poetry. Symbols are pictures that represent bigger ideas. For instance, the symbol for love might be a heart, and a symbol for America might be a flag.

Directions: Look at the list of topics. Create a symbol that might represent each concept. Draw your symbol in the box.

1. Use inside voices.	**2.** Science is amazing.
3. Clean up after yourself.	**4.** Friendship is the best.

Directions: Now let's take this idea one step further and create a shape poem. A shape poem forms the outline of a particular shape or symbol. The shape says something about the poem's topic. For example, a poem about love might be in the shape of a heart.

On a separate piece of paper, create a shape poem about a topic. Make the shape of the poem represent the ideas that the words of the poem express.

Designing a Call to Action

Project-Based Writing Connection: When stating your position on an issue, it is often necessary to include a solution that makes sense.

One of the most important parts of a persuasive essay is your proposed solution. You have to get your reader to want to do something as a result of learning about your issue.

A "call to action" does that. It calls a group of people together to act on solving a problem. There are many different ways to do this. Here are some methods:

❖ **Debate** — You can have each side present its case in the form of a civil argument.

❖ **Rock-Paper-Scissors** — Have two people compete in a winner-take-all format.

❖ **Compromise** — Each side can give up a little so that a middle ground is reached and everyone "wins."

❖ **Petition** — You can influence an outcome by getting a lot of people to back you up.

❖ **Vote** — You can take a vote, and the majority wins.

Directions: Decide on which method you would like to ask your reader/audience to use in order to solve the problems below. Say why you would choose that method.

Statement of Opinion	Call to Action
1. We should be able to bring water bottles to class.	Method: _____ Why?: _____ _____
2. There should be a stop sign put in at the corner near the park.	Method: _____ Why?: _____ _____
3. We should have a local book swap on the first Saturday of every month.	Method: _____ Why?: _____ _____

Conducting a Movement Survey

Project-Based Writing Connection: This activity will help you do research by gauging public opinion about a topic.

In this activity, your class will vote on issues with their bodies by moving to different areas in the classroom. This offers you a quick, visual way of "taking the temperature of the class" on important issues. After conducting the survey, hold a class discussion about the results. This will allow your classmates to explain their choices.

Tip: Conduct the survey twice: once *before* your classmates learn more about the topic (in order to gauge prior knowledge), and once *after* you have presented evidence about the topic (in order to see if their opinions have changed).

For example, imagine that the topic is "dress codes in school." Let's say you are already researching the pros and cons of a school dress code, but you would like to know the opinion of the class before you present any evidence to them.

Here is some language that you can use to conduct a movement survey:

Before you all came into the classroom, I put up two signs: one says "Pro," and the other says "Con." You can see them on either side of the room.

The topic I'm going to be discussing is whether or not schools should have a dress code.

On my signal, you can vote by standing under the sign that matches your opinion.

❖ If you believe that there is a reason that schools should have a dress code, please quietly go stand under the "Pro" sign.

❖ If you believe, without a doubt, that schools should not have a dress code, then go stand under the "Con" sign.

❖ If you are undecided, please go stand in the middle of the two groups in the back of the room.

Directions: Use the form on page 35 to conduct a movement survey in your classroom. Reference the cheat sheet provided on page 34 in order to lead a respectful, informative classroom discussion about the results of the survey.

Conducting a Movement Survey *(cont.)*

After conducting the movement survey, you can then lead the class in a discussion about the results. When you permit the participants in the survey to give their rationale for choosing the sides they did, this will provide you with further evidence for your research project. Take notes on what people say, and write down direct quotes whenever possible.

When conducting the discussion part of your survey, it's important to allow one side to talk and the other side to respond *to that point alone*. This is called "refutation," and it is a vital part of a persuasive counterargument. A back-and-forth exchange of dialogue on a key point might look like this:

Student A: A dress code works because it puts us all on an even level of appearance.

Student B: That's an interesting point, and I agree that it evens things out, but it doesn't allow for individuality and diversity in appearance.

Use this cheat sheet to keep the discussion respectful and on track:

Here are some guidelines your classmates should keep in mind:

- ❖ You are agreeing and disagreeing with points, not with people.
- ❖ If you disagree with a point, that doesn't mean the point isn't important.
- ❖ People are more likely to listen if you are respectful and listen to them.

Here are some sentence stems for discussion:

To disagree:
- ❖ I realize not everyone will agree with me, but . . .
- ❖ That's an interesting idea, but maybe . . .
- ❖ I see it a little differently because . . .

To agree:
- ❖ I agree with what _____ said about . . .
- ❖ I was wondering/thinking about that, too.
- ❖ Can I just take that point a step further and say that . . .

To encourage participation:
- ❖ We haven't heard from you yet.
- ❖ Could you give me an example of that?

To add to the thought:
- ❖ May I add something here?
- ❖ Maybe you could . . .

To clarify:
- ❖ Could you repeat/rephrase that?
- ❖ In other words, you think that . . .

Conducting a Movement Survey *(cont.)*

A movement survey is a way for you to conduct a poll by asking people to stand in a place that represents their opinion on a topic.

Step 1:

On the day *before* the activity, write down a little information to read to your pollsters to give them the context of your topic:

* ❖ Write one sentence that argues **FOR** a side: _____

  _____

* ❖ Write one sentence that argues **AGAINST** that side: _____

  _____

* ❖ Write a question you want to ask your pollsters: _____

  _____

Step 2:

On the day of the activity, hang a sign in the room on one wall marked "PRO." Put a sign marked "CON" on the opposite wall. You can decorate your sign with symbols about your topic.

Step 3:

Read your information to your pollsters to give them information on your topic.

Step 4:

Ask students to go stand under the sign that best represents their opinion.

Step 5:

Ask people to give other reasons why they believe the way they do. If you write down the best argument you hear word-for-word, you can use the quote as evidence in your essay.

Number of students who stood under the **PRO** sign: _____

* ❖ The best argument from the **PRO** side: _____

  _____

Number of students who stood under the **CON** sign: _____

* ❖ The best argument from the **CON** side: _____

  _____

Use the information above for your research, advocacy, or persuasive essays.

Writing a Recipe for "Success"

Project-Based Writing Connection: Use the format and elements of recipes to examine a theme or topic in a unique way.

We all know what the average recipe looks like, but have you ever thought of using that format to describe the ingredients of something that you couldn't touch or that wasn't meant to be eaten?

Recipes usually include a few standard elements and often look like this:

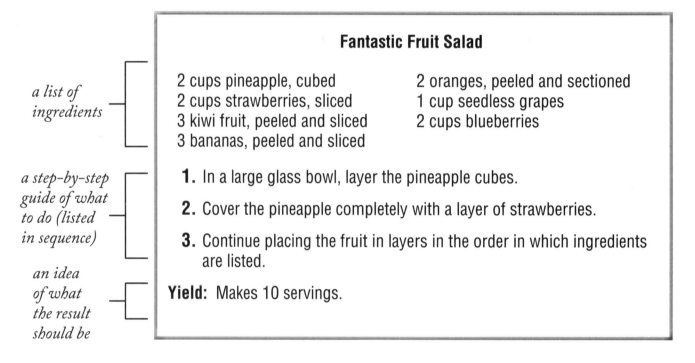

a list of ingredients

a step-by-step guide of what to do (listed in sequence)

an idea of what the result should be

Fantastic Fruit Salad

2 cups pineapple, cubed   2 oranges, peeled and sectioned
2 cups strawberries, sliced   1 cup seedless grapes
3 kiwi fruit, peeled and sliced 2 cups blueberries
3 bananas, peeled and sliced

1. In a large glass bowl, layer the pineapple cubes.

2. Cover the pineapple completely with a layer of strawberries.

3. Continue placing the fruit in layers in the order in which ingredients are listed.

Yield: Makes 10 servings.

What if, instead, you were to use the traditional recipe format to describe what goes into something more abstract, like "imagination" or "success"? You would first need to ask yourself the following questions:

❖ What are the ingredients that make up this abstract idea?

❖ How much of each ingredient is required?

❖ How many will the recipe serve?

❖ What are the stove settings and the cooking times?

Directions: Complete "Cooking Up a Convincing Story" on page 37. Create a recipe for something that can't be eaten or touched. Follow the format shown above.

Cooking Up a Convincing Story

Sometimes it takes planning to get what you want. You have to think of the best way to go about persuading someone to do something for you or give you something. Do it the wrong way, and your hopes will be dashed. But follow the perfect recipe, and your wish might just be granted.

Directions: Imagine that you want something from someone, and all you have to do is come up with the perfect recipe to make it happen. Fill out the form below. What — and how much — will it take?

Sample Idea: "How to Get Your Sibling to Let You Use His/Her Video-Game System"

How to _____

Ingredients:

❖ 4 cups of _____

❖ 3 tablespoons of _____

❖ 2 pounds of _____

❖ 1 pinch of _____

Directions for Cooking:

_____

_____

_____

_____

_____

_____

_____

Yield: _____

Using an Illuminated Letter

Project-Based Writing Connection: You can use an illuminated letter to add a visual element to represent your topic in the final draft of a written piece.

An *illuminated letter* is an illustration of a letter, often the first letter of chapter or book. Symbols and icons are drawn into the letter as a way of giving visual hints to the reader. They give the reader an idea about the text that follows.

For instance, let's say that someone was looking at a book of Peter Pan. The first line of that book is as follows:

   "All children, except one, grow up."

In this case, the "A" in "All" might look like the letter to the right:

Directions: Look at the illuminated letters below. On the lines next to each, predict the name of the fairy tale in which this letter might appear.

   _____
                        _____

   _____
                        _____

Now, let's practice this concept by creating an illuminated letter based on a topic you know a lot about: yourself. Using the first letter of your first name, create a block letter in the space to the right. Then design and fill the rest of the space with symbols that represent you.

Using an Illuminated Border

 Project-Based Writing Connection: To visually tie a project together, add a border around the final drafts of your writing.

Much like an illuminated letter, an *illuminated border* can be used to add visual meaning to a written piece. However, by using the margins of a document, an illuminated border frames the text. It creates a decorative picture around the page. This allows the artist to depict not only symbols, but also landscapes or scenes, much in the same way a comic-book artist of today will sequence a story.

Remember, the illuminated border always stays focused on the main idea of the text.

Directions: Look at the page below. Inside the page, there is a paragraph about theme parks. In the framed border surrounding the paragraph, create an illuminated border that captures the main idea of the paragraph.

Creating a successful theme park is more complicated than it looks. Designers think long and hard about their guests. They must consider more things than just rides and food. There are pathways around the park. There are ways in which people line up for rides. There are trashcans, restrooms, gift shops, and more. So much needs to go into creating a theme park. So the next time you are at a theme park, look down. The path on which you are walking was imagined by someone who was thinking all about you.

Creating a Comic Strip

 Project-Based Writing Connection: Use the format of a comic strip (brief text, illustrations) to highlight the important points in a narrative.

You have probably read (and enjoyed) a comic strip. But did you realize that a comic strip is a perfect multi-genre project? After all, it combines pictures and writing.

Begin this next activity by reading this story:

The Knight and the Skeletons
by Ben Gawron

Once upon a time, there was a prince and a wizard. The king had left his magic sword for his son, the prince. The prince, however, was too scared to carry it and hid the sword in a chest so nobody could use it. The evil wizard came searching for the magic sword. He looked all around—under rocks, over walls, under bridges, and around trees. As he looked, he froze the townspeople with his freezing spell.

The prince heard of his people being frozen and decided he needed to do something. He opened the chest. It had cobwebs on it because it hadn't been opened in a long time. He lifted the sword and promised to be brave. The sword gave him strength. There was a mighty battle, and the wizard was captured.

Directions: Begin this assignment by highlighting the three most interesting or important lines in the story. Then draw these moments in the boxes below. Imagine that you are zooming in on one important detail for each moment.

Creating a Comic Strip *(cont.)*

Directions: Use the frames below to create a comic strip based on your topic. First, you have to decide what are the most important elements of the story or argument to draw. Then, you have to decide on the visual style of your drawing.

Here is a list of elements to focus on:

Story Elements	Writing Devices	Camera Angles
❖ plot	❖ hook	❖ close-ups
❖ setting	❖ sequence	❖ ¾ shots
❖ characters	❖ suspense	❖ long shots
❖ descriptions	❖ foreshadowing	❖ foreground vs. background
❖ conflict	❖ zooming in on a moment	
❖ resolution	❖ dialogue	
❖ theme		

Making a Flip Book

Project-Based Writing Connection: A flip book is a great way to show — both textually and visually — a sequence of steps or events.

A flip book is a mini-project that includes both writing and art in order to describe a sequence of steps or events. These steps can form a how-to description, a summary of a novel, a timeline, etc. The different pages of the flip book can also be used to illustrate the different elements of a complex issue.

In order to make a flip book, you need these materials:

- ❖ several sheets of paper
- ❖ stapler
- ❖ drawing supplies
- ❖ pen

Then, follow these steps:

1. Stagger several sheets of paper in order to create visible tabs.

2. Fold the sheets to create a booklet of consistently spaced tabs.

3. Staple the booklet's folded edge.

4. On the cover, give your flip book a title (the name of the book, the name of the process being described, etc.). Also write your name.

5. Label the tabs by section or chapter.

6. Fill in your summaries, responses, and art.

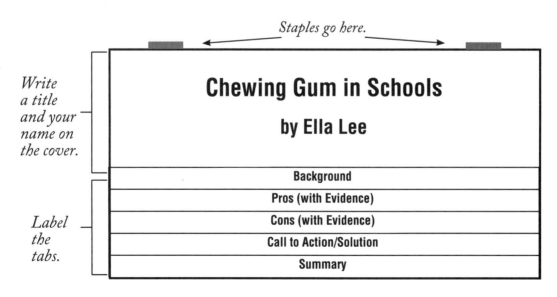

Reading and Writing a Script

Project-Based Writing Connection: Use the script format to create characters who are affected by or talking about a topic or theme.

A script is a written version of a visually performed medium (a play, a television show, a movie, etc.). It includes the dialogue, a setting, and stage directions.

Here's an excerpt from a script for a sci-fi movie called *Alien in the Bathroom*.

(PETE brushes his teeth in the morning. He looks tired and groggy. Suddenly, a head pops up out of the toilet. PETE screams.)

PETE
Ahhhh! What? Who?

ALIEN
(looking around)
Is it safe to come out now, human? Are the GSA nearby?

PETE
The who? What are you talking about? And what are you doing in my toilet?

ALIEN
I'm hiding from the Galactic Space Authorities. My spaceship crashed into the sewer at the edge of town, and I've been swimming upstream ever since!

(PETE is speechless. He tries to reach for his toothbrush — which he had dropped into the sink — but he's unsuccessful. He can't take his eyes off of ALIEN.)

PETE
(backing away as ALIEN begins to climb out of the toilet)
Whoa. Wait.

ALIEN
(grabbing a towel and drying himself off as if nothing unusual is happening)
Relax, human.

Writing a script takes the following elements:

1. the character names (in all caps)   **3.** the dialogue (not in quotation marks)

2. the directions (in parentheses)

Directions: On a separate sheet of paper, continue the scene by having the two characters exchange some new lines of dialogue. Remember to include the three components — character names, stage directions, and dialogue — formatted properly.

Using Technology to Present

 Project-Based Writing Connection: Add extra appeal by using a 21st-century, technology-based method to present your project.

These days, we don't just explain what we know through oral presentations or the traditional book report; we use technology to display and communicate our knowledge. Think about what you would want to watch or listen to or read, and then go ahead and create that for your work. Listed below are three possible ways you can display what you've learned in a method that reflects the age you live in, the Age of Technology.

❖ **Set Up a Screencast** — Using an iPad app like Educreator or ShowMe, you can display an image and record narration. You can then submit it from your tablet directly to the website. A link will be provided, which you can submit to your teacher for viewing.

Example: Let's say your project involves designing your own country. Open up a screencasting app and draw the map of your country. Include borders, the most important cities, and symbols to represent geographical features. Narrate as you draw so that your viewers can hear your description of the country.

❖ **Produce a Prezi** — A Prezi uses a concept map rather than slides to go from idea to idea. What's unique about a Prezi is that you can load an image that represents your whole topic and then "zoom in" on the details that show off your knowledge on that topic. If you go to *http://prezi.com*, you can see examples of this cool presentation software. You can create your presentation for free, and it's stored on the Web, always there for your teacher to access it.

Example: If your project is about saving an endangered species, you can upload an image of the animal and zoom in on specific features.

❖ **Make a Movie** — There are so many ways to create a digital movie. Whether you are using iMovie on a Mac or producing a free, Web-based, 30-second movie using Animoto, you have options.

Example: Find visuals to represent each step of your project. Upload them into Animoto, add some copyright-free music from a site like *www.Soundzabound.com*, and watch a 30-second narrative of your work in pictures and music. Send the link to your teacher.

Directions: Let's say your subject is texting while on the move (walking, riding a bicycle, riding a skateboard, etc.). Think about your position on this activity. Then think about which of the above methods would be the best way to give a presentation on this subject. Give a complete answer on a separate piece of paper.

Wrapping It All Up

Project-Based Writing Connection: A container provides an attractive way to present your final project and tie all of its individual elements together.

Finding a visual way to present your project is important when getting ready to turn in the final results. The package or container in which you house your work is another opportunity to show what you know. It's like the punctuation at the end of the sentence or the glue that holds it all together. It's a visual way to really send home your message with your audience.

Directions: In the activity below, draw lines to match the container with its appropriate topic. The first one has been done for you.

Pizza Box with essays inserted inside	Pollution
Clothes Hanger with essays dangling below at different levels	Body Image
Mailbox with a collage of essays taped onto its surface	Childhood Obesity
Rolled Scrolls tied together with a ribbon and quill	Getting Rid of the Post Office
Trash-Can Lid with essays glued to the inside	The History of the Amendments

Now, what containers would you pick for the following topics?

1. Protecting Endangered Species _____

2. Global Warming _____

3. Library Closures _____

Ask Yourself: What container could you use to house your own project? How would that container help your audience connect with your topic?

Bibliographies

Project-Based Writing Connection: This resource shows you how to cite the information used in research projects. (Blank forms are on page 47.)

Every research essay needs evidence, and every piece of evidence comes from somewhere. It's important, therefore, to learn how to create a proper bibliography.

Bibliography Cheat Sheet

Book

Author's last name, first name. *Book title.* City of publication: Publishing company, Publication date. Pages. Medium.

Example:

Blume, Judy. *Superfudge.* New York: Dutton Children's Books. 12–23. Print.

Article in a Newspaper or Magazine

Author's last name, first name. "Article title." *Periodical title.* Month, Year: Pages of actual article. Medium.

Example:

Smith, John. "Dancing with the Cars." *Car and Driver Monthly.* April, 2003: 12–14. Print.

Website

Author. Date. "Name of article." *Name of website.* Date retrieved and where retrieved from (URL).

Example:

Delbanco, Andrea. May 6, 2011. "A Modern Fairy Tale." *Timeforkids.com.* Retrieved on July 5, 2011 from *http://www.timeforkids.com/.*

Interview

Subject's last name, first name. Personal Interview. Date of interview (day, month, year).

Example:

Spielberg, Steven. Personal Interview. 14 January 2011.

Movie

Title. Name of director. Year of release. Format. Studio, release date of format.

Example:

E.T: The Extraterrestrial. Steven Spielberg. 1982. DVD. Universal Studios, 2005.

Bibliographies *(cont.)*

Directions: Use these forms to record information as you gather research. You may not be able to fill in every line, depending on the information available.

Information Source: Book

Author's Name: _____

Title of Book or Selection: _____

Series Title: _____

Editor or Translator's Name: _____

Edition and Volume Number: _____

Publisher: _____

Publication City and Date: _____

Page Numbers: _____

Information Source: Periodical (magazine, newspaper, etc.)

Author's Name: _____

Title of Article: _____

Title of Periodical: _____

Series and Volume Numbers: _____

Publication Date: _____

Page Numbers: _____

Information Source: Internet

Author's Name: _____

Title of Article or Page: _____

Name of Website or Company: _____

URL: _____

Publication Date (or Date Last Revised): _____

Access Date: _____

Taking Notes

Project-Based Writing Connection: This resource can help you organize and process information for any project.

When you research information, you need to find a way to organize it. Cornell notes are a great way to do this. These notes are divided into three main sections:

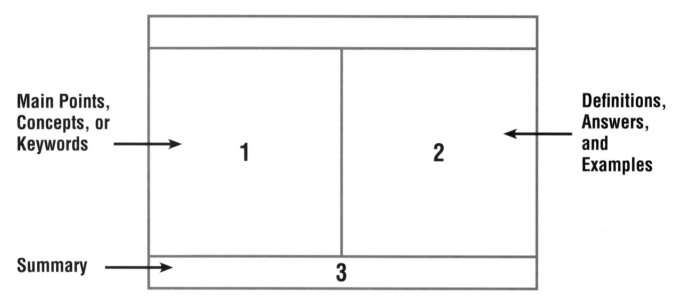

Here is a brief description of those sections:

1. **Main Points, Concepts, or Keywords** — Record this information in the left-hand column on the page. Main ideas and key elements (dates, people, etc.) should be included here. Also use this space to develop questions that need to be answered about the topic.

2. **Definitions, Answers, and Examples** — This information should be recorded in the right-hand column. Use this large space to explain the terms and answer the questions listed on the left. Be brief and clear. Use bullet points or short phrases. Skip lines between ideas.

3. **Summary** — A brief summary of the topic and your finding should be recorded here. Aim to summarize the information in three sentences or less.

You can use these instructions to create your own Cornell notes on a piece of lined paper, or you can use the blank template provided on page 49.

Taking Notes *(cont.)*

Directions: Use this template to help organize your research about your topic.

Name:	Date:
Topic:	Class:
Main Points, Concepts, or Keywords:	**Definitions, Answers, and Examples:**

Summary:

Outlines

 Project-Based Writing Connection: The resources on pages 50–53 can help you get organized before you begin writing an essay.

The outline on this page focuses on helping you write a narrative, or story.

A **narrative/story** is a piece of writing or speech that describes a sequence of events. A narrative can be completely fictional (like a fantasy) or based on truth to some degree. It includes any kind of story—from science fiction to love stories to personal memoirs.

Here are some elements to look for when reading and revising narratives:

I. The Opening (Exposition)

   A. Hook

   B. Characters

      1. Physical Traits

      2. Personality Traits

   C. Setting

   D. Main Story Conflict

II. The Body (Rising Action — Climax — Falling Action)

   A. Sequential Events (or flashback if using that strategy)

   B. Sensory or Emotion Details (sight, smell, touch, taste, sound, feel in your heart)

   C. Foreshadowing/Suspense

   D. Figurative Language (simile, metaphor, onomatopoeia, personification, etc.)

   E. Dialogue

   F. Description of Facial Expression, Gestures

   G. Transitions

   H. Action Verbs

III. The Ending (Resolution)

   A. "Tie it all up"

   B. Lesson Learned, Theme, Moral, Motto, etc.

Hint! Remember to incorporate these six traits of good writing for added sophistication:

❏ Sentence Variety   ❏ Proper Conventions   ❏ Great Ideas

❏ Voice   ❏ Word Choice   ❏ Organization

Outlines *(cont.)*

The outline on this page focuses on helping you craft a **persuasive** essay. This type of writing is meant to influence and change minds. Being able to write a successful persuasive essay is an important skill. Use the strongest word choices and evidence in order to increase your chances of convincing your readers.

Here are some elements to look for when reading and revising persuasive writing:

I. Introduction
  A. Hook
  B. Background Information
  C. Who is affected by this issue?
  D. Thesis Statement (Opinion + Reason #1 + Reason #2)
  > For instance: *I strongly believe that the school vending machines should only sell water because it is a healthy alternative to sugary drinks and it costs less.*

II. Body paragraph: Reason #1
  A. Main Topic Sentence (general statement)
  B. Expansion of the Main Topic (gets more specific)
  C. Textual Evidence/Proof (quotes, statistics, data, personal experience, etc.)
  D. Commentary/Connection to the evidence
  E. Transition to next paragraph

III. Body paragraph: Reason #2
  A. Main Topic Sentence (general statement)
  B. Expansion of the Main Topic (gets more specific)
  C. Textual Evidence/Proof (quotes, statistics, data, personal experience, etc.)
  D. Commentary/Connection to the evidence
  E. Transition to next paragraph

IV. Counterargument
  A. Main Topic Sentence (states the opposing side's *best* point)
  B. Expansion of the Main Topic (gets more specific)
  C. Textual Evidence/Proof (quotes, statistics, data, personal experience, etc.)
  D. Commentary/Connection to the evidence
  E. Conclusion that *refutes* this point (i.e., why it doesn't convince you)

V. Conclusion
  A. Reiterate Thesis (using different words)
  B. Solution/Call to Action (what we should do about it)

Outlines *(cont.)*

The outlines on this page focus on two different types of essay: the summary and the reading-response.

A **summary** is a brief overview of a piece of writing. It gives a reader the most important points. The key in writing a summary is to make it simple so that it is easily understood.

An outline of a summary might look like this:

I. Main Topic Sentence

    A. Include the writing's title, author, and genre.

    B. Keep this sentence general.

II. Most Ideas

    A. Only use the most important points.

    B. Don't use small details.

    C. Use transitions.

    D. Go in chronological (time) order.

    E. Don't use voice.

    F. Use sentence variety.

III. Conclusion

    A. Quickly restate main point.

    B. Don't give your opinion.

A **reading-response** essay lets you write about something you have read. You might use it to explain your personal feelings about a book or to give your thoughts about what the author was trying to say.

An outline of a reading-response essay might look like this:

I. Introduction

    A. Hook

    B. Background information

    C. Main topic sentence

II. Body Paragraphs

    A. Reasons supporting your main topic sentence

    B. Quotations that illustrate your reasons

    C. Explanations of what the quotations mean and how they support your point

    D. Graceful transitions

III. Conclusion

    A. Main topic sentence restated and explained

    B. Parting thoughts

Outlines *(cont.)*

The Story Swoop

Directions: Use the story swoop to organize your narrative. Write in the most important parts of your story in the appropriate places along the swoop to show how your narrative flows from one idea to the next.

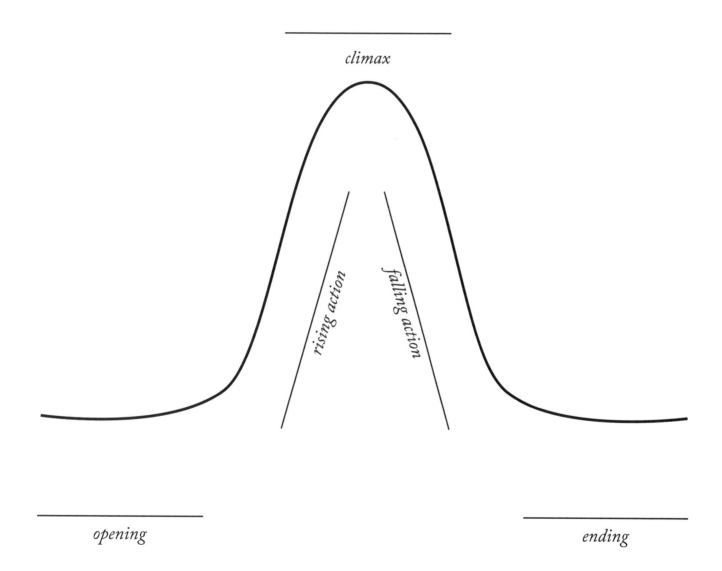

climax

rising action *falling action*

opening *ending*

The Writing-Genre Chart

 Project-Based Writing Connection: This resource can get you thinking about different forms of writing.

Directions: Study the chart below, which shows some elements that go into four different genres of writing: Narrative, Summary, Persuasive, and Response to Literature.

Teacher Note: This chart is meant to get students thinking about the overlap in writing genres. The categorization of some of these elements may be up for debate. Use this resource to spark a classroom discussion about writing.

Genre	Narrative	Summary	Persuasive	Response
Hook (grabbing the reader's attention from the beginning)	√		√	√
Main Topic Sentence (tells what the writing will be about)		√	√	√
TAG (title, author, genre)		√		√
Evidence (proof, quotes, data, etc.)			√	√
Transition Words (these help the writer move from sentence to sentence)	√	√	√	√
Sentence Variety (sentences that are both long and short, simple and complex)	√	√	√	√
Conventions (spelling, grammar, mechanics, etc.)	√	√	√	√
Sensory Details (sight, sound taste, smell, touch)	√			
Plot (what happens in the story)	√			
Setting (description of location)	√			
Characters (traits and qualities)	√			
Conflict (the problem in story)	√		√	
Theme (moral, message, lesson)	√	√		
Call to Action (solution to problem)			√	

Unit Checklist

Project-Based Writing Connection: A checklist can help you organize your time and your work so that you never lose sight of your deadlines.

Here are some tips for using this checklist.

❖ In the "Assigned Element" column, fill in a more general type of element, like "Research" or "Written Piece" or "Visual Element."

❖ Use the "Possibilities" column to think of ways you could meet those requirements, like "Survey" for research or "Movie Poster" for visual element. Try to jot down a lot of ideas in the "Possibilities" column.

Date Due	Date Done	Assigned Element	Possibilities

Using Rubrics

 Project-Based Writing Connection: Rubrics can help you understand what is expected of you before you begin each part of a project.

A rubric is a chart. It serves two important purposes:

1. Before you start a project, a rubric can give you an idea of what you are expected to do on that project.

2. Once you are finished with a project, a rubric can give you a score and tell you why you earned that score.

There are three basic steps needed to make this kind of chart:

Step 1: <u>In the left-hand column</u>, list the qualities that you believe are the most important in order to do well on the project.

Step 2: <u>Across the top</u>, list the rankings that would describe how well a person did. Do this by writing a number and a word. For instance, you could write a "5 – Fantastic" in the first box, and you could write "1 – Poor" in the last box.

Step 3: <u>In the boxes of the chart</u>, write descriptions of what the different scores would look like. Use words that you know.

Here is an example of a rubric:

	4 (Awesome!)	**3**	**2**	**1**
Word Choice	My words are the best options. I tried hard to find the best word for the job.	My word choices are good but not always the best. They are at my grade level.	My words are simple and to the point, with no creative choices.	I repeat a lot. My words are definitely below my grade level.
Sentence Fluency				
Organizations				
Ideas				

Writing Reflection

Project-Based Writing Connection: At the end of any project, it's important to look back at what it took to create your final product.

You've gone through a long and crazy process of creating this project, so now it's time to take a moment to think about how far you've come and what it took to get here.

Directions: When you are ready to turn in your final draft, sit down and reflect on the following five questions. Answer these questions honestly, then staple this response sheet to your checklist (if you've been using one throughout this project) and include it as your final piece of writing in your project-based writing project.

1. How did I think about my audience as I created this project? _____

    _____

    _____

2. A lot of skills went into this project. Create a list of at least four skills that you used to make this project what it is. _____

    _____

    _____

3. What parts of this project do I find the weakest? _____

    _____

    _____

4. Did I take any risks? Did I try anything new to create this project? Explain your answers. _____

    _____

    _____

5. What do I hope my reader will learn from exploring my project? _____

    _____

    _____

Unit 1: Teach the Teacher

Teacher Instructions

"Teach the Teacher" is a multi-genre unit that asks each student to select a topic for a course that he or she will teach to the class. This unit is all about the power of student choice. It puts the authority of the lesson in the students' hands. It leads them through the process of thinking of a unique lesson to teach and then designing it. Ultimately, this unit will prepare each student to present an entire lesson and assessment to the whole class. In the process, their knowledge of these topics will reach new heights. After all, knowing content is important, but being able to communicate it involves a much deeper understanding of the content.

Begin the lesson by having students consider topics that they might want to teach. Instruct them to choose topics with which they are familiar but about which they can learn more through research. Then have them list the pros and cons of each topic they are considering until they can narrow their choices down to that one special topic that they are excited to share with the class.

This unit includes the following components:

❖ **"A Topic to Teach"** (page 59) — Have students do research and submit persuasive pitches that explain why their topics are worthy of being taught.

❖ **"Create a Lesson Plan"** (pages 60–61) — Begin this activity by showing an example of a lesson plan. Then have your students create outlines for their own lesson plans.

❖ **"Quiz the Class"** (pages 62–63) — Examine the different types of quiz questions before having students create quizzes based on their teaching topics. (Note: Before distributing these pages, locate an appropriate quiz-making website. Sign up for an account, if needed, so that your students can use the website to create quizzes online.)

❖ **"Give an Oral Presentation"** (pages 64–66) — Give students tips on the why's and how's of planning a successful oral presentation, which they will then use to present their topics to the class.

❖ **"Write a Persuasive Letter"** (page 67) — Direct students to write a business letter to a school administrator; this letter will explain why their topic should be considered as a possible new elective for the following school year.

❖ **"Unit Checklist"** (page 68) — This valuable resource keeps students focused, on task, and in front of deadlines.

A Topic to Teach

Have you ever wanted to teach a lesson? Have you ever wanted to teach your classmates something they never knew before? Well, you are going to be given the chance to do just that! But first, you have to get your idea approved by your teacher.

Begin by writing your topic here: _____

Directions: Use the following outline to help you think of the best way to convince your teacher that your topic is worthy of being taught.

I. **Hook** — Begin your essay with a sentence that will grab your teacher's attention.

_____

_____

II. **Background Information** — Pretend your teacher knows nothing about this topic. Write one or two sentences to give him or her some background on the subject.

_____

_____

III. **Thesis Statement** — Write a statement that says what you want to study and why. Use the following format:

I want to be permitted to research _____ *because* _____.

Give two reasons why this topic is fascinating to you.

_____

_____

_____

IV. **Counterargument** — Give a one-sentence counterargument that acknowledges why your teacher might not allow you to spend time researching your topic.

_____

_____

V. **Your Response** — Write one sentence that speaks directly to your teacher's concerns, and convince him or her why you should still be permitted to continue with your subject.

_____

_____

Create a Lesson Plan

In order to engage learners, you need a plan. Many teachers design formal lesson plans for each lesson in order to break down how to best communicate their content to the class. You will now create a plan that includes these elements:

- ❖ **Objective** — What is the specific skill that you want your class to know? What is the broader lesson that you will be teaching?

- ❖ **Materials** — List the things you will need to conduct your lesson. This is not only for you, but also for your teacher so he or she can provide you with the items.

- ❖ **Step-by-Step Lesson** — Give some thought to what you will do first, second, third, etc., as you walk through the lesson.

- ❖ **Check for Understanding** — Develop some questions to ask students as you progress through your lesson to make sure that they are "with you."

- ❖ **Assessment** — Create and distribute a quiz to assess how well your students listened, as well as how effectively you presented your material.

Here is a sample lesson plan that follows this outline:

Objective: I want my class to learn about the history of toasters.

Materials:

- ❖ toaster
- ❖ poster
- ❖ computer
- ❖ PowerPoint
- ❖ bread
- ❖ LCD projector

Step-by-Step Lesson:

Step 1: Introduce materials.

Step 2: Talk about how people used to toast bread before toasters were invented. Give name of inventor. Use PowerPoint presentation to explain how first toasters operated. Show how they evolved into the options we have now.

Step 3: Toast bread.

Step 4: Describe what's happening as the bread toasts. Explain how the toaster does it.

Check for Understanding:

1. Ask, "What else do you use toasters for?"

2. Ask review question: "Who invented the toaster?"

3. Ask, "Could someone share with us what kind of toaster he or she has at home?"

Assessment: Distribute a 5-question quiz to students.

Create a Lesson Plan *(cont.)*

It is your turn to create a lesson plan that will help you teach your topic to the class.

Directions: Follow the outline below to create a rough draft of your lesson plan.

Objective: _____

_____

Materials:

Step-by-Step Lesson (only fill in as many steps as are needed):

Step 1: _____

Step 2: _____

Step 3: _____

Step 4: _____

Step 5: _____

Step 6: _____

Step 7: _____

Check for Understanding:

1. _____

2. _____

3. _____

Assessment: _____

Quiz the Class

Have you ever wanted to develop your own quiz? Now is your chance. And as an added bonus, you might find that by designing questions for your classmates to answer, you will learn even more about the topic.

You are going to develop a 5-question quiz on your topic. In order to do this, let's first look at the different formats for the questions that make up quizzes.

Here are the three different kinds of questions you can ask:

❖ A **choice** question is one that "forces" the test-takers to choose a particular answer. Multiple-choice, true/false, and matching questions fall under this category.

Example: *Tinkerbell is a unicorn. True or false?*

❖ An **order** question asks how you would rank something. Asking for someone to give a star rating or a letter grade are examples of **order** questions.

Example: *Do you think that the cafeteria serves tasty food? Give a score of "5" if the food is delicious or a "4" if it's just really good. A "1" score means you think the food is awful.*

❖ An **essay** question allows the test-taker to develop the entire answer.

Example: *At the end of Stellaluna, the little bat finds her mommy. What do you think would happen if the little bat always lived with the birds?*

Directions: On a separate piece of paper, create your own quiz based on your lesson presentation. Your quiz should have five questions. It should be made up of the following types of questions:

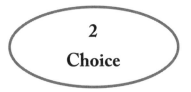

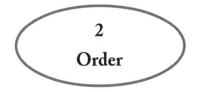

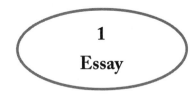

21st-Century Connection: With your parents' or teacher's permission, go online to *www.surveymonkey.com*. There, you can design an online quiz. Your classmates can take the quiz, and the website will score the results.

Quiz the Class *(cont.)*

Directions: Look at the questions and decide if they are **Choice, Order,** or **Essay.** Then, explain why you believe the way you do. The first one has been done for you.
Hint: Only answer the "What type of question is it?" and the "Why?" questions.

Question #1. Should vending machines with soda and candy be allowed in school?
- ❏ Yes, students have the right to choose what they eat and drink.
- ❏ No, school vending machines should be filled with healthy drinks and snacks.

What type of question is it? _____Choice_____   Why? <u>I am only given the two choices, I'm forced to choose between the two.</u>

Question #2. How should my school handle the long lunch lines? Rank from 1 to 4 ("1" = best and "4" = worst).
- _____ Stagger the lunch times.
- _____ Allow students to earn "Front of the Line" privileges.
- _____ Create more server windows.
- _____ Sell food in carts, as well as in the cafeteria.

What type of question is it? _____   Why? _____

_____

Question #3. Which statement best describes how you feel about global warming?
- **A.** I don't think it will happen.
- **B.** People and governments should act now to try to prevent or prepare for it.
- **C.** The world may change, but living creatures will adapt.
- **D.** There's nothing we can do about it.

What type of question is it? _____   Why? _____

_____

Question #4. What are the ways you need to prepare your home for a new pet?

What type of question is it? _____   Why? _____

_____

- -

Teacher Note: Fold this section under to cover it before making copies.
Answers: **2.** Order; **3.** Choice; **4.** Essay

Give an Oral Presentation

Great speakers don't just magically know how to present well. They practice.

When you practice your oral presentation, you need to be aware of lots of things.

Directions: Cut out the reminder card below. Bring it up to the front of the class with you and put it where you can see it as you present. Use it to remind yourself what you need to be aware of as you speak in front of an audience.

- ❖ On this page, you will find a helpful "Presentation Reminders" card that you can use on the day of your speech to help keep you focused and on track.

- ❖ On the next page, you will find many tips to help you time your presentation.

- ❖ On the third page, you will find a template for your presentation.

Begin by writing an outline of your presentation. Base this outline on the lesson plan you have already created. Once you've written your outline, then the real rehearsals begin. Use the reminder card below. Use it to help you practice your speech. You can also bring it up to the front of the class with you and put it where you can see it as you speak.

Presentation Reminders

Volume

Can your audience (your *whole* audience) hear you? Remember to **speak loudly** enough so that the person at the back of the room can hear you.

Emphasis

Are your words flat and monotone, or is there emotion in your voice? How many "um"s, "er"s, or moments of silence are there in your presentation? Are you mumbling? Remember to **speak clearly** and show emotion.

Stance

Are you leaning, fidgeting, or rocking? Remember to **stand up straight**.

Eye Contact

Are you using your eyes to connect with your audience? Or are you staring at your notes? Remember to **look at people** in different parts of the room.

Content

Did you do your research and are you communicating that research? Remember to **stay on topic**.

Timing

Are you speeding? Remember to **speak as if you're telling a story**.

Give an Oral Presentation *(cont.)*

Timing is important when you are speaking in front of an audience. It takes rehearsing your oral presentation over and over in front of a mirror for yourself, for your family, or for your friends.

Start by writing bullet points or an outline on cards. Then begin to present your lesson. As you do this, pretend your audience is in front of you.

Directions: Below is an activity that will aid you in timing out your presentation perfectly. Follow the steps provided.

Step 1

Create an outline of your content. Base this outline on your lesson plan.

Step 2

Grab a timer.

Step 3

Stand up and use this worksheet as a cheat sheet as you time your presentation one section at a time.

Step 4

Slow down! Don't be nervous, and be sure to stay in control of your speed rather than the speed being in control of you. It might feel weird, but do it in slow motion once all the way through. Then try it again at a normal pace. This will help you avoid going too fast.

Step 5

With each attempt, write down your time next to the section to indicate your speed and pacing. Get it consistent, and you're ready to go.

Step 6

Repeat. Do it over and over until you don't need the timer to tell you how long you are spending on each section.

Give an Oral Presentation *(cont.)*

Directions: Below is one possible oral presentation broken down into sections. Chunk your presentation into sections, and time each section using the template below.

Hook

1st time through: _____   2nd time through: _____

Did you slow down with each rehearsal? Circle your response.   **YES**   **NO**

Background Information

1st time through: _____   2nd time through: _____

Did you slow down with each rehearsal? Circle your response.   **YES**   **NO**

Main Content

1st time through: _____   2nd time through: _____

Did you slow down with each rehearsal? Circle your response.   **YES**   **NO**

Questions & Answers (practice with someone asking you questions and you responding)

1st time through: _____   2nd time through: _____

Did you slow down with each rehearsal? Circle your response.   **YES**   **NO**

Administer Quiz (giving instructions)

1st time through: _____   2nd time through: _____

Did you slow down with each rehearsal? Circle your response.   **YES**   **NO**

At the end of each full presentation, add your totals together.

1st time through: _____   2nd time through: _____

Reflection

❖ Which was your best time? _____

❖ Why do you think it went better than the other times? _____

Write a Persuasive Letter

The final piece of writing in this unit is a business letter you will write to the principal of your school. In other words, you are going to try to convince your principal to do something. The letter pulls together everything you've done and uses it to help you convince your principal that your topic should be a class at your school.

To do that, you need to write a persuasive essay in the form of a business letter. Remember your writing skills, remember your audience, and remember to be persuasive.

Follow the format below:

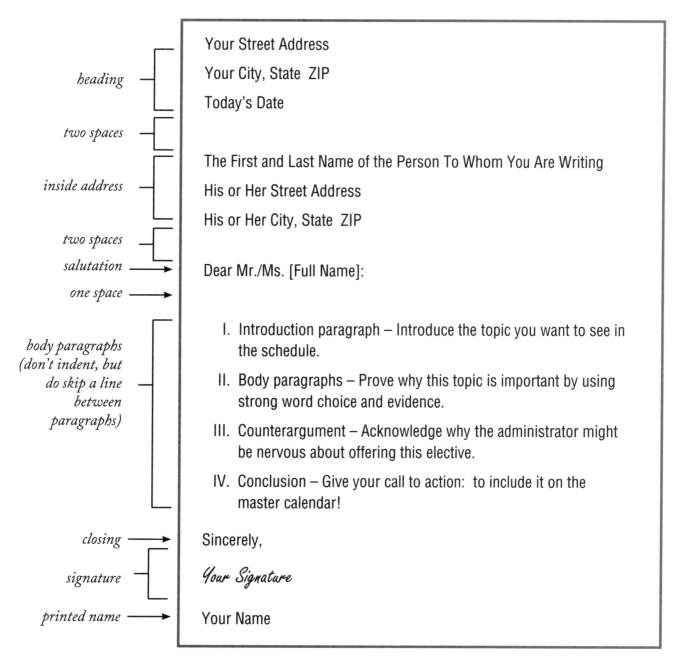

heading

Your Street Address

Your City, State ZIP

Today's Date

two spaces

inside address

The First and Last Name of the Person To Whom You Are Writing

His or Her Street Address

His or Her City, State ZIP

two spaces

salutation

Dear Mr./Ms. [Full Name]:

one space

body paragraphs (don't indent, but do skip a line between paragraphs)

I. Introduction paragraph – Introduce the topic you want to see in the schedule.

II. Body paragraphs – Prove why this topic is important by using strong word choice and evidence.

III. Counterargument – Acknowledge why the administrator might be nervous about offering this elective.

IV. Conclusion – Give your call to action: to include it on the master calendar!

closing

Sincerely,

signature

Your Signature

printed name

Your Name

Unit Checklist

Below is a possible checklist for the "Teach the Teacher" unit. It should help to organize your time and work as you move through the process of creating a full project. Look ahead on your checklist and never lose sight of deadlines!

Genre	Description	Due	Turned In
1. Persuasive Writing	Write a persuasive business letter to your teacher pitching your topic.		
2. Lesson Plan	This is a step-by-step description of what you will teach, what you will need, and the activities that you will be doing with the class.		
3. Quiz	A 5-question assessment using various questioning strategies that the class will take and you will grade. (The score will not be counted against your classmates.)		
4. Bibliography	Include a works-cited page. Use correct bibliographical format.		
5. Oral Presentation	This will be scored using the oral-presentation rubric.		
6. Visual or Kinesthetic Element of Presentation	This can be an activity you are asking the students to do or a visual element used during your lesson plan (poster, PowerPoint, props, etc.).		
7. Container	How are you going to present your project? What will it look like?		

Unit 2: Persuasive-Writing Project

Teacher Instructions

The aim of this unit is two-fold: to teach students to write persuasively, and to encourage students to connect school life to real life. Writing persuasively is at the heart of any advocacy research essay. It is also at the heart of this project-based writing unit that gives students the freedom to choose a topic to study and the format in which they want to persuasively present their results.

Now, it can be difficult for students to choose a topic to feel strongly about. Help guide them to think about their communities close to them (their school, their neighborhood) and those farther away (another town, state, or country). Some students are ready to think about global issues, while others need to just focus on those within their own school site. Let them choose topics that they feel passionately about, and they will become fledgling advocates for bigger issues in the future.

This unit includes the following components:

❖ **"Consider Cause and Effect"** (page 70) — Get students thinking about causes and their effects. This will help them to look at their topics from more angles and examine the impacts these topics can have on the world.

❖ **"Targeting a Topic"** (pages 71) — Have students narrow down their choices for a topic that interests them. As they do this, students will consider the impact their topics have on the world. (Note: You may want to distribute copies of this worksheet so students can fill them out for multiple topics.)

❖ **"All in One Sentence"** (page 72) — Show how a thesis statement functions, and have students create thesis statements for essays about their topics.

❖ **"Two Kinds of Graphs"** (page 73) — Discuss the functions of graphs and examine two important types (the bar graph and the pie chart).

❖ **"Giving Great Interviews"** (pages 74–76) — In this activity, you will first give students tips and ideas for conducting great interviews. Next, you will give them practice interacting with the person they are interviewing.

❖ **"Unit Checklist"** (page 77) — This valuable resource keeps students focused, on task, and in front of deadlines.

Consider Cause and Effect

It's important to understand that when an action takes place, there are always consequences. In other words, when something happens, there are results that occur because of that happening. This is called "cause and effect." Here is an example:

Action (Cause)	**Consequence (Effect)**
A student studies hard.	The student does well on his test.

Directions: The chart below gives some causes and effects. Fill in blank boxes with appropriate responses. There are not necessarily any right or wrong answers. Just think about what makes sense.

Cause	**Effect**
A boy sneezes and doesn't cover his mouth.	
	The creatures in the oceans begin to die.
More people begin sharing rides to work every day.	
	Everywhere we walk, we get gum on our shoes.
With every "A" a student gets, she gets $1 from her school's program.	

Take a look at the topics below. Decide if you are interested in discovering more about their causes and/or effects. Circle the ones that interest you most.

- traffic
- rainforests
- arts in schools
- dissecting animals
- money for grades

- money for attendance
- commercials aimed at children
- dress codes in schools
- gum-chewing

- cell phones in schools
- texting
- earning allowance

Targeting a Topic

Directions: It's time to choose a topic that is important and interesting to you. Fill out the following worksheet for a subject that you might want to focus on. Choose a topic that you think you will enjoy learning about.

Topic: _____

List three facts you already know about this topic:

1. _____

2. _____

3. _____

Now, list one PRO (positive thing) about the topic and one CON (negative thing) about it.

Pro: _____

Con: _____

Next, answer the following questions about the topic:

1. Why is this issue important? Why should your audience learn about it?

   _____

   _____

2. Why are you interested in this topic? How do you think you relate to it?

   _____

   _____

3. Finally, think about the effects of this topic. Who does it impact? Is it important to the entire world or just to your school or town? Explain your answer here.

   _____

   _____

All in One Sentence

In one sentence, a thesis statement tells the reader what the essay will be about. For a persuasive essay, it gives the author's opinion and the reason(s) for his or her beliefs.

Here is a thesis statement for an essay about students having water bottles at their desks:

     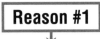

I strongly believe we should be able to keep a water bottle at our desks in class because drinking water keeps us hydrated during the day.

Directions: Look at the thesis statements below. For each one, do the following:

❖ Underline the phrase that states the author's opinion.
❖ Draw a box around the phrase that gives the author's reason for feeling this way.

Thesis Statement #1

We should start a recycling program at our school because it would create awareness about the amount of paper we waste each week.

Thesis Statement #2

We students should participate in the PTA's fundraiser because the money is going to help children our age.

Directions: Now think about a possible thesis statement for the topic you've chosen. Fill in as much information as you can before writing your thesis statement below.

Your topic: _____

Your opinion: _____

Your most important reason: _____

_____

Your thesis statement: _____

_____

_____

Two Kinds of Graphs

Have you heard the saying "A picture is worth a thousand words"? An image can often convince a reader more than only words would. Graphs give a great way to do just that. Two of the most common are the bar graph and the pie chart.

A *bar graph* uses rectangular bars to show the values of the things they represent. Bar graphs are great for showing the difference between values. For example, look at the data given for a project on gum chewing. Use the results to fill in the bars on the graph below. The first bar has been done for you.

Question: "What do you do with gum when you're done chewing?"

Results (in number of students):

"I don't chew gum." = **6**

"I throw it in the trash." = **15**

"I swallow it." = **9**

"I spit it on the ground." = **3**

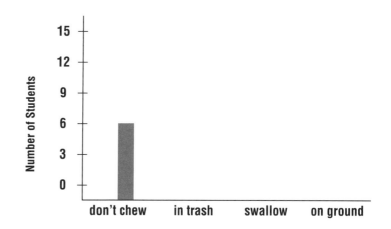

A *pie chart* is in the shape of a circle that is divided into sections. Pie charts are great for showing big differences when your data is far apart.

For example, look at the results of a TV poll and use them to label the sections of a pie chart. The first one has been done for you.

Question: "How much television do you watch each week?"

Results (in number of students):

10 hours or more = **60**

5–9 hours = **12**

1–4 hours = **6**

I don't watch TV = **2**

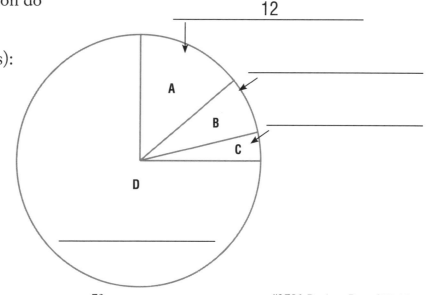

Giving Great Interviews

For a research project, you might want to interview someone who can give you some information that you wouldn't be able to find out in a book or online. You want the subject to respond in a unique way you wouldn't find anywhere else.

To get a great interview takes planning. There are two stages to conducting an interview. Here are tips to help you get the most out of both of those stages:

Interviewing Tips
The Preparation

☞ Research your topic thoroughly.

☞ Research your interview subject and how he or she relates to your topic.

☞ Bring a pen and paper — or better yet, a way to record the subject's voice.

☞ Come to the interview with a list of at least 10 questions. Make sure they are not "yes or no" questions.

☞ When you initially contact the person for an interview, don't assume that he or she has the time or the desire to meet you. Be polite and ask if he or she would be so kind as to give you some time.

☞ Arrive dressed for success.

☞ Be on time.

Interviewing Tips
The Actual Interview

☞ Use eye contact.

☞ Shake the interviewee's hand in greeting and when saying goodbye.

☞ Say "Thank you."

☞ Ask a question that you've prepared, then listen to the response. A good rule of thumb would be to ask a follow-up question based on the response. This proves you are paying attention to the person's response and not just thinking about your next question.

☞ When the interview is over, go somewhere where you can write/type everything that you remember, even if you've recorded the interview. Note the person's clothes, the room, and the walls — everything that can serve to set a scene for those who read your interview.

Giving Great Interviews *(cont.)*

Directions: In the following activity, you are going to practice asking interview questions based on an answer you are given.

Interview #1

Imagine you are interviewing the principal of your school. The topic of your project is "Paying Students for Good Attendance." You ask the following question:

"Would you ever pay a student for coming to school?"

Here is the principal's answer:

"Well, I would say that good grades are a form of payment, right? The way I see it, if students don't come to school, then they won't have an opportunity to earn that good grade. Paying students just for showing up doesn't help them. When I was a student, my parents would pay me a quarter for every "A" I got, but my school wasn't involved in that reward. Should schools be involved in that kind of praise?"

Based on the principal's answer, write two questions you could ask to prove that you were listening to the response.

1. _____

2. _____

Interview #2

You are interviewing a local bookstore manager about why the store is closing. You ask the following question:

"Why do you think the store is closing?"

Here is the manager's response:

"I think we just couldn't compete with that big store that opened up down the street. They carry every book imaginable, while we only carry science fiction and fantasy. Pretty soon, fewer and fewer people came in. It got so bad that we just had to start packing up our boxes. I'll miss this ol' store. It was started by my dad years ago."

Based on the manager's answer, write two questions you could ask to prove that you were listening to the response.

1. _____

2. _____

Giving Great Interviews *(cont.)*

The Thank-You E-Mail

After you have conducted an interview, you need to write a thank-you letter to the person who gave you his or her time. You can handwrite it or write an e-mail.

Directions: Pretend that you are writing a project on "Why Kids Need to Learn Internet Skills Earlier." You interviewed your friend's father, who works at a computer store.

Use the e-mail form below. Follow these guidelines in your thank-you e-mail:

❖ Use a polite greeting.

❖ Remind him of the interview.

❖ Mention one point he made that was particularly helpful.

❖ Thank him again and sign the e-mail with your full name.

To:

From:

Subject:

Unit Checklist

Below is a possible checklist for the "Persuasive-Writing Project" unit. It should help to organize your time and work as you move through the process of creating a full project. Look ahead on your checklist and never lose sight of deadlines!

Genre	Description	Due	Turned In
1. Persuasive Writing	Write a persuasive business letter to your teacher in which you give your idea for a topic.		
2. Research	Use at least two different sources, plus one interview.		
3. Narrative	Write a short story based on your topic.		
4. Bibliography	Include a page that cites the places where you found information.		
5. News Article	Write a news article about your topic. It must include a visual (picture, graph, etc.), as well as text.		
6. Persuasive Writing	Write an essay that convinces your audience of your opinion and gives a solution to the problem.		
7. Container	Use a container that houses your project and contributes to its overall message.		

Unit 3: Create-a-City Project

Teacher Instructions

Most research reports ask students to study a topic — for instance, their home city — and regurgitate what they've learned. But the highest form of comprehension is not in being able to remember (after all, we live in the age of the search engines, right?), but in being able to create something from the information we understand. Researching a city is one thing, but imagining a whole new city is another, far-more creative endeavor. In 3rd grade, students study the many elements that go into a city or town. The following project-based writing unit will take this one step further and ask students to create an entirely new city located somewhere in their home state.

From a student's perspective, the act of creation makes learning more engaging. From a teacher's perspective, it makes the process of guiding students more engaging, too.

This unit includes the following components:

❖ **"City Search"** (page 79) — Begin the unit by having your students complete this word search. By doing so, they will reinforce their knowledge of some of the parts that make up a city.

❖ **"Put Your City on the Map"** (pages 80–81) — After practicing their mapping techniques on a smaller scale, students will create maps of their cities.

❖ **"The Facts About Your City"** (page 82) — With this activity, students will think more deeply about their newly created city and what makes it unique.

❖ **"Read All About It!"** (pages 83–84) — After learning about the parts of a newspaper article, students will create the front page of their city's newspaper.

❖ **"A Great Place to Visit!"** (page 85) — Through the creation of travel brochures, each student will have the opportunity to convince readers why his or her city is the place to visit. A travel brochure serves as a great project-based writing activity because it combines genres by incorporating visuals, narratives, and facts all in one handy, folded document.

❖ **"Unit Checklist"** (page 86) — This valuable resource keeps students focused, on task, and in front of deadlines.

City Search

Before you begin creating your own city, it might help to remind yourself of some of the things that most cities and towns need.

Directions: Locate the "City Terms" in the word search below. As you do, think about how these parts help make up a city.

City Terms

BANK
CITY HALL
FIRE STATION
HOSPITAL
LIBRARY

MALL
MARKET
NEIGHBORHOODS
PARKS
POLICE STATION

POST OFFICE
RESTAURANTS
ROADS
SCHOOLS

```
                P               E                               P
      C         A               C                       B       O
      I    T    R          Y    I          C    T       A       L
 B    A    N    K          O    F          L    I       S    C    H
 A    R    P    S     L    O    F    F    M    A    R    K    E    T
 N    E    I    G    H    B    O    R    H    O    O    D    S    Y
 J    O    U    R    E    S    T    A    U    R    A    N    T    S
 S    L    C    H    H    O    S    P    I    T    A    L    A    M
 D    O    S    C    H    O    O    L    S    O    O    F    T    A
 A    O    D    R    T    A    P    Y    R    A    R    B    I    L
 O    O    H    S    C    I    T    Y    H    A    L    L    O    L
 R    I    F    I    R    E    S    T    A    T    I    O    N    L
```

Extra Assignment: On the back of this paper, write sentences that include the city terms from the word search.

Put Your City on the Map

Maps are all around us. You can find a map of a country, a state, a town, even your school. Many times, maps are laid out like a grid.

Directions: Try mapping your own classroom. Think about it from a bird's perspective looking down. Where are the desks in relation to the board? Are there computers? Where is the classroom library? Use the grid below to show where everything is.

	A	B	C	D
1				
2				
3				
4				

Now, describe where an object is by naming the grid box in which it appears. For example, if a desk appears in the top, left-hand corner, you can say that it can be found in (1-A).

Where are these objects or places on your map?

1. your desk _____

2. the main door _____

3. the front of the classroom _____

4. a computer _____

5. a friend's desk _____

6. a bookshelf_____

Put Your City on the Map *(cont.)*

In many cities, the buildings are laid out in a grid. What this means is that the streets run parallel and perpendicular to each other.

❖ Parallel lines travel in the same direction and never intersect.

❖ Perpendicular lines intersect, forming square corners.

Directions: Think about the city you are creating. Fill in the grid below with a neighborhood. Cut out the buildings at the bottom of the page and place them on the map. Also, name the streets so you can give directions to any visitor to your city.

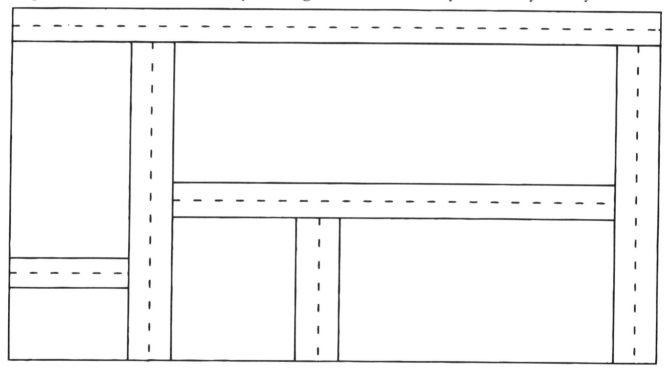

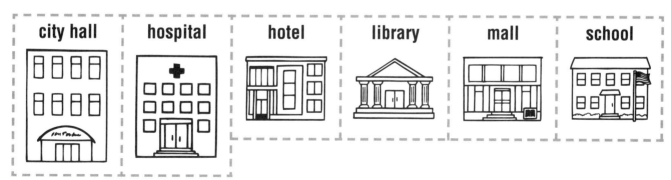

city hall   hospital   hotel   library   mall   school

Additional Activity: On a separate sheet of paper, write step-by-step directions guiding a visitor to the local library from the hotel.

The Facts About Your City

Directions: Fill in the following fact sheet about your city or town. Use this sheet as a guide as you write your narrative.

1. What is the name of your city? _____

2. Did the name come from somewhere? Does it mean something? Explain.

   _____

   _____

3. How many people live in your city? _____

4. In which state is your city located?_____

5. Is there dramatic topography (for example, a canyon, a mountain range, a river, a desert, etc.) that runs through your city?

   _____

   _____

6. What sports can you play in your city using its natural topography?_____

   _____

7. What industry does your city specialize in? _____

8. What is the single biggest tourist attraction in your city? _____

   _____

9. What is your mayor's name? _____

10. What are two facts about your city that make it unique to this country?

   _____

   _____

Read All About It!

A newspaper or online feature article is a perfect project, all wrapped up in one place. It usually combines writing, photographs, graphs, interviews — you name it.

A newspaper article has a specific structure. It typically has five components:

1. **Headline** — This is the title of your article. It quickly grabs the reader's attention and tells him or her what the article is about.

2. **Byline** — This names the author of the article.

3. **Lead Section** — These intro paragraphs tell the reader the most important parts of the story. The first paragraph contains a *hook* to grab the reader's attention. The section continues with the "Five Ws and One H" (Who, What, When, Where, Why, and How) about the subject.

4. **Expansion** — These are the next few paragraphs that build on the first paragraph. This is where the reader can learn about what people have said about the topic. Perhaps there are details like quotes or data to back up the topic of the article.

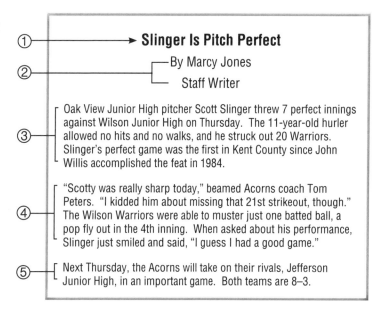

5. **Related Information** — This includes additional information that might prove interesting to the reader but that isn't important to understanding the initial purpose of the article.

Directions: Find a newspaper article or an online article. (A good place to look online is at *http://www.timeforkids.com*.) If you are using an online article, cut and paste it into a word-processing document and print it out. Use highlighters to mark each part of the article that answers one of these questions:

Who – blue		**Where** – yellow	
What – green		**How** – pink	
When – red		**Why** – orange	

Read All About It! *(cont.)*

Directions: In the following activity, you are going to begin creating a front page of your town's local newspaper. For your paper's front page, include the following articles:

- ❖ **feature article** — This should describe a current event that is going on in your town.

- ❖ **op-ed article** — This is an opinion piece. In it, you give your opinion about a key topic of debate happening in the city. This should persuade your reader to agree with your opinion.

- ❖ **entertainment article** — This can be about anything to do with the world of entertainment. Is there a movie opening in your town? Was there a celebrity sighting recently?

- ❖ **sports article** — Write about your city's favorite pastime or about an event that will be going on this coming weekend.

- ❖ **your choice** — Use your imagination to come up with an article that is all your own.

You can begin by sketching the layout of your front page in the space below. Include your paper's name and its logo. Then draw and label boxes showing where each of your articles will fit on the front page.

A Great Place to Visit!

When tourists go on vacation to an unfamiliar place, they often look at travel brochures in order to find out more information about that place. Brochures are like handy reference guides that tell about places to go, locations to visit, facts about the area, and restaurants to try. Best of all, the wealth of information found on a travel brochure can be folded up and fit conveniently into a pocket for easy reference.

Directions: It's time to create a travel brochure for your city. It all starts simply with a piece of 8½" x 11" paper folded to look like the image to the right:

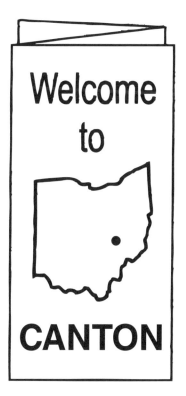

Here are some guidelines to follow as you create your travel brochure:

On the front . . .

❖ Write the name of the city.

❖ Include a drawing, photo, or other visual that represents the city.

On the inside . . .

❖ Include information that will grab your reader's attention and really convince him or her to visit your city:

    • unique places to see   • quotes from visitors and citizens

    • facts about the city   • restaurants to try

    • pastimes to enjoy   • sports teams to watch

As you fill in the details of your brochure, remember to make persuasive word choices. After all, you are trying to build excitement and interest in your city. You are trying to show why it is a great destination spot for travelers.

Unit Checklist

Below is a possible checklist for the "Create a City" unit. It should help to organize your time and work as you move through the process of creating a full project. Look ahead on your checklist and never lose sight of deadlines!

Genre	Description	Due	Turned In
1. Persuasive Writing	Create a tourist brochure designed to persuade tourists to visit your city.		
2. Research	Complete at least two pages of notes about your real city or town.		
3. Fact Page	Submit a completed form that gives all of the general information about your mythical city.		
4. Map	Complete a map of your imaginary city. Include a key, symbols, and a compass.		
5. Multi-Genre Writing	Design and create a front page for your city's newspaper.		
6. Your Choice	Choose an additional genre to depict your topic.		
7. Container	How are you going to house your project?		

Unit 4: Create-a-School Project

Teacher Instructions

We know that creating is a higher-level skill than merely reporting. In that spirit, have the students think about the place where they learn and then take it a step further by designing their own school. What classes would be offered? What food would be served in the cafeteria? What would the campus look like?

In the "Create a School" project-based writing unit, students are asked to role-play as the architect, the principal, the superintendent, a teacher, etc. Students get to make the decisions themselves, thus owning their own learning a little more than before.

This unit includes the following components:

❖ **"Clue In to School"** (page 88) — Begin the unit by having your students complete this crossword puzzle. By doing so, they will reinforce their knowledge of some of the parts and people that make up a school.

❖ **"What Makes a Great School?"** (page 89) — In preparation for creating their own schools, students should use this activity to jot down ideas about the qualities that make up a great school.

❖ **"Your School Rules"** (page 90) — Have each student create a constitution by which his or her school will operate.

❖ **"A Landscape of Learning"** (page 91) — In this activity, students get a chance to create visual maps of their campuses, complete with building, play areas, and anything else they wish to include in their schools.

❖ **"Making Class Goals"** (page 92) — Students will not only decide which classes will be taught at their school, but also what the learning objectives are for each class.

❖ **"Words To Learn By"** (page 93) — Next, students will create a motto that encompasses the main objective of their schools.

❖ **"Home of the Best Crest!"** (page 94) — Have students exercise their visual creativity by creating logos that represent their schools.

❖ **"www.Your_School"** (page 95) — Each student will create a homepage for their school's website.

❖ **"Unit Checklist"** (page 96) — This valuable resource keeps students focused, on task, and in front of deadlines.

Clue In to School

Do you know the names for everything at your school? Before you design your own school, you should really know what the proper words are for some of its parts.

Directions: In the crossword puzzle below, identify the correct words for the school-related clues. Choose your answers from the words in the box.

campus	constitution	motto	science
classes	crest	principal	students

Across Clues

1. the grounds (buildings, outdoor areas, etc.) of a school

5. a set of rules by which a school (or country, etc.) is run

6. along with math, English, and social studies, this is one of the four CORE subjects

8. the name for courses in which learning takes place

Down Clues

2. the person who is in charge of a school and who oversees its day-to-day operations

3. the people who are at a school to learn and to be taught

4. a saying or slogan by which a school tries to operate

7. a logo that is designed to represent a school

What Makes a Great School?

As you begin to think about the school you would like to create, it's important to start by thinking about the qualities that go into a great school.

Directions: Answer the questions below to help you as you design your school. Use them to brainstorm the features that your imaginary school will have.

1. When a student walks into your school, what will he or she immediately see?

   _____

2. Besides classrooms, what other buildings make up the school?

   _____

3. What will the inside of each classroom look like?

   _____

4. About how many students will be in each class per teacher?

   _____

5. Other than core subjects (English, math, science, social studies), what classes will be offered?

   _____

   _____

6. What will be the daily schedule of a typical student?

   _____

   _____

   _____

7. Name two afterschool clubs that will be available.

   _____

8. What will the play area look like?

   _____

9. How are students to be dropped off or picked up?

   _____

10. Finally, what is the name of your imaginary school?

    _____

Your School Rules

Our country has a constitution that describes some of the key rules by which we live as citizens. A classroom or school can also develop a constitution.

Directions: Pretend that you are a principal of your school, and you are developing a constitution by which all of your students and teachers will learn and work.

In the document below, develop 10 key rules that will help run your school. Try to keep them positive. After all, a whole list of "Don't do this" and "Don't do that" becomes boring. Instead, focus on how to get the best out of students in terms of behavior and academics.

The Constitution of _____
(name of your school)

1. _____

2. _____

3. _____

4. _____

5. _____

6. _____

7. _____

8. _____

9. _____

10. _____

A Landscape of Learning

Think about schools and the way they are built. Here is a list of elements that a typical school might have:

classrooms	snack stand	fences
library	benches	playground
main office	pathways	field
nurse's office	grassy areas	track
cafeteria	trees	courts

There are many other possibilities. Your school might not have some of what's on this list, or it might have even more.

Directions: In the space below, draw an overhead map of your school. Include as many elements as you can. It's time to reveal the layout of your exciting new school.

21st-Century Connection: The drawing above can serve as a rough draft for your project. Consider using a computer program (such as Google SketchUp) to create a more professional-looking map. Or, try creating a 3-D sculpture using any kind of material you can think of. There are so many possibilities.

Making Class Goals

What subjects do students take at your school? What are the objectives that a student must learn? An objective is like a goal. This is an important part of any school.

For example, here is a short list of objectives for a 3rd-grade writing class:

Students will learn to

* ❖ *write clear and understandable sentences*
* ❖ *write about a main idea*
* ❖ *participate in the writing process (prewriting, rough drafting, revising, editing, final drafting, and presenting)*

Directions: Look at the following list of subjects. Think about what students should learn in these classes. Create a short list of objectives (at least two) for each subject being offered at your school. For the last one, choose a subject that isn't listed.

Reading _____

_____

Math _____

_____

Science _____

_____

Social Studies _____

_____

P.E. _____

_____

_____ _____
(your choice)

_____

Words To Learn By

A school theme, or motto, is a saying that describes the overall qualities of the students or school. Here are some examples:

Excellence Through Study	**The Future Starts Here**	**Caring, Sharing, Daring**

Each of these mottos helps to tell visitors a little something about the place it represents.

Directions: Draw lines to match each motto with the school it describes.

1. Discovering the Gifts in Every Child	This school believes that students should be willing to give everything a try.
2. Try Everything	Students at this school know that if people dedicate themselves to learning, their lives will be richer.
3. Learning to Live, Living to Learn	This school recognizes that every student has something special inside.
4. Acceptance, Attendance, Application	The students at this school are tolerant, come to school daily, and apply themselves every day.

It's time to create a motto for your school. Think about the qualities that you want your students, teachers, staff, and families to have.

First, write down three adjectives to describe your students. _____

_____

_____

Next, write down a brief description of what you want your school to represent.

_____

_____

Use these ideas now to create your school motto. Write it on the line below:

_____

Home of the Best Crest!

Some schools have a visual logo, or crest, that represents them. This crest is made up of symbols that represent important qualities that the school possesses. It sometimes appears on everything from their letters to their uniforms to the banners around school.

Directions: Design a crest for your school. Begin by thinking about your school motto (page 93) and about the kinds of pictures and symbols that can show what these words mean. Also, carefully consider the color of your crest.

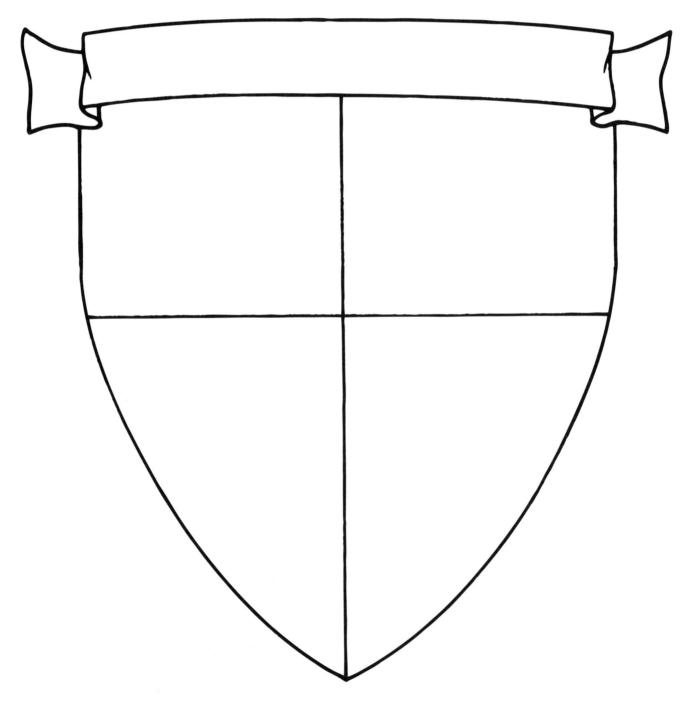

www.Your_School

A website is the ultimate multi-genre project because it includes text and visuals. A school website is important because it give parents, students, and visitors an idea of what the school has to offer.

Directions: In the following activity, you are going to create a homepage for your imaginary school's website. You may want to begin by examining your own real school's website and seeing the elements that it has already. Think about what you like or what you would change. Once you've made those decisions, you need to create a rough-draft sketch of what your homepage should look like.

Be sure to include a banner, which usually runs along the top of a web page. A banner might include the name of your school, your school's motto, and a visual that represents your school. It is often the first thing that catches the eye of someone who is seeing your website.

21st-Century Connection: With parents' or teacher's permission, you can go online and easily create a free website using *www.weebly.com*.

Unit Checklist

Below is a possible checklist for the "Create a School" unit. It should help to organize your time and work as you move through the process of creating a full project. Look ahead on your checklist and never lose sight of deadlines!

Genre	Description	Due	Turned In
1. Persuasive Writing	Give a persuasive speech to the Board of Education about what makes your school a great place for learning.		
2. Research	Complete at least two pages of notes based on your actual school.		
3. Narrative	Write a short story set in your mythical school.		
4. Visual	Design a blueprint of your school in either a 2-D or 3-D medium.		
5. Directional Writing	Create a constitution of rules for your students to follow.		
6. Visual	Design a crest for your school.		
7. Informational Writing	Create a homepage for your school's website.		
8. Container	How are you going to house your project?		